THE CURRENCY TRADER'S HANDBOOK

Strategies for Forex Success

Rob Booker

For Kris and Isaac and William

Preface

Who are you?

I have absolutely no idea who you are, what you do for a living, if you trade only currency, or futures, or livestock, beanie babies, cold cereal, your best friend's vinyl Rush collection (please, does anyone else think that Getty Lee sounds like a dying cow?), or your wife's fine china.

I do know that if you have traded currencies, that you have probably lost some money here and there, and I hope this handbook is of some help to you. If you have never lost money trading currencies, then I want you to close this book, open your trading account, produce last month's report, and then vomit all over yourself.

Oh, and none of the people depicted in this book are real. Well, I'm real. And my wife is too. And my cat is real too, although she is technically not "people."

P.S.S. For a free trial of my nightly forex report, point your browser to:

http://www.robbooker.com

Introduction

You can trade for a living. Really. You can.

The question people ask me most often is, not surprisingly, "Can I be successful at this?" Mostly, they ask me the question after a devastating loss. It's a natural time to ask the question, but it's a horrible time to answer it yourself.

Why? Because you can be successful, and every time you start to feel depressed about losing, you stop believing in yourself. If you stop believing in yourself, you stop working as hard, and if you stop working as hard, you start to make more mistakes, and a vicious cycle begins. Losses bring depression which brings more losses, and then before you know it you've lost your entire first account.

You don't have to trade that way. There is a better way to trade.

I trade currency for a living, and so can you. Maybe it will take you more than a year to become successful. Maybe more. But you can do it. You don't have to be better than most people at math. You don't have to score high on an IQ test. You don't have to be the smartest person you know.

You just have to be disciplined.

This book is includes:

1. Revised editions of ebooks that I have written over the years. Each of them has been downloaded from my website tens of thousands of times.   I've dusted them off, re-written them, added new material — all with the intent to share with you what has helped me to become a successful trader.

2. New material that has never been published before, including the chapter on testing; the chapter on the 10 rules of trading, and the picture of the smoking monkey, which has no purpose at all but it made me laugh.

3. A new edition of *The Miracle of Discipline.* This section is larger than all the other chapters of this book, but this version of the essay is actually edited to bring you only the most important concepts. You're going to hear me say this a million times, and I will say it here to start it off: in trading, discipline matters more than anything else. Period.

I hope that you will share with me your successes and your failures. You can contact me by visiting my website: http://www.robbooker.com or by email:

rob@robbooker.com

I answer every email I receive. Sometimes it takes me a while to answer them all, but I do. On the website, I try to place as much free content as possible. Stop by sometime.

Rob Booker
Wheeling, W.Va.
January 2006

Contents

Come Into My Trading Bathroom   1

Strategy:10   9

The Role of Confidence   21

Dr. Spock on Trading   29

The Woodchuck and the Possum   35

The Miracle of Discipline   43

The 10 Rules of Trading   67

Oh, Crap! I Lost All My Money!   73

5/13/62   81

Why I Teach   95

Chapter One

Come Into My Trading Bathroom

When you read a book by Alexander Elder, he invites you into "his trading room." When you come into *my* trading room, you're really coming into the bathroom. In fact, the subtitle of this introduction ought to be: *A Complete Guide to Flushing Your Profits Down the Toilet.*

I learned how to trade the hard way. By losing. Over and over. Think of a stupid mistake that traders make: I made that one. Think of another one: I made that one too. Only by keeping excellent records, staying determined, and learning from my mistakes was I able to being to trade profitably on a consistent basis. But along the way I learned that if you would rather flush your profits down the toilet, you should do the following things:

1. Trade as much as possible. Trade all the time.
2. Never close a losing trade.
3. Always close a winning trade as quickly as possible.
4. Never test a trading system. Trade it live ASAP.

5. Fund your first live account with all of your savings.

6. Fear losing, winning, trying, failing, and succeeding.

7. Ignore the trend.

8. Don't ask someone better than you for help.

Anyway, you get the idea. I did all of this stuff, and much more. Boy, I was really stupid. But that's all over now. Once I turned the corner to profitability, I never looked back.

THE BASICS

Before we get into specifics, I want to make sure you have a basic knowledge of currency trading. You might want to skip this section if you know what a pip is, how margin works, and that kind of stuff.

THE CURRENCY MARKET

The currency market is by far the most liquid and largest financial market in the world. More than $1.5 trillion USD is traded in the worldwide currency market *every day*. That is at least 15-20 times bigger than all of the equities markets in the United States and Europe combined.

Over 90% of all daily transactions involve trading of the Majors, which include the US Dollar, Japanese Yen, Euro, British Pound, Swiss Franc, Canadian Dollar and Australian Dollar.

The currency markets only "close" on Saturdays, meaning there is little or no trading at all during that time — remember, most of the heavy trading is done by banks, which do not have open trading desks on Saturday. However, from Sunday morning Eastern Standard Time (which is already the start of the week in Asia), through Friday at about 5:00pm Eastern Standard Time, traders are moving the market.

Hedge funds have become huge players in the currency markets, as the US stock market has simply not given these firms enough chances to stay in trades (many hedge funds stay in some type of trades all the time). Currency markets tend to be more volatile (i.e., they move more), so active traders, such as hedge funds, can move in and out of trades nearly as often as they wish.

In currency trading, there is no central exchange – so all trading occurs in what is called "over the counter" trading – where buyers and sellers match themselves up through various dealers or directly to each other on the banking trading systems. Two prominent trading platforms for banks and hedge funds are Reuters and EBS.

Banks, hedge funds, and bigger traders execute trades using a the "Interbank" system – meaning, they look for buying and selling opportunities from each other directly, using a Reuters or EBS (or other) platform. These platforms allow them to see current prices, usually with a very tight spread of 1-3 pips on the majors. One other unique feature on these robust trading platforms is that traders can see orders to buy or sell *outside* the current market price. If a bank trader wants to buy $100 million Euros, they can literally pick up an order for the entire amount from another bank trader someplace else — usually at a price slightly different from the current market price.

Individual speculators, like you and I, trade using a dealer like GFT, Oanda, or HotspotFX. When you place an order with a dealer, that dealer usually immediately takes the other side of the trade. Your dealer is NOT matching your order up with another trader in their system. That is practically impossible, because you are trading such small amounts.

I repeat: when you buy 1 mini lot (more on that later) of GBP/USD, your dealer is selling you 1 mini lot of GBP/USD. Your dealer is not matching you up with another trader who wants to sell you some British Pounds.

Don't be alarmed that your dealer takes the other side of your trade. If they didn't, then you would not be able to trade at all unless you had a significant amount of capital. Don't assume that because your dealer takes the other side of the trade that he is going to stop you out and take your money.

Imagine if your dealer screwed everyone in the system by doing this all day long. How many clients would that dealer have? While some dealers are better than others (email me at rob@robbooker.com for some reviews of dealers), it should not be hard for you to find one that you really feel comfortable with.

CURRENCY PAIRS

A currency pair is a combination of two currencies. Let's use a commonly traded currency pair as an example. If this is the first time that you have broken a currency pair down into its separate parts, it might be a bit confusing. Read this over a couple of times if you need to, or send me an email. So here it is, a currency pair:

GBP/USD

The above pair is the abbreviation for the Great British Pound versus the United States Dollar. The currency mentioned first in the pair (GBP in this example) is called the "base" currency. If the GBP/USD quote is 1.9000, then one British Pound will buy 1.9000 dollars.

When you buy the GBP/USD, you are betting that the GBP is going to move higher. That automatically means that the US Dollar is moving lower. Duh, right?

If the GBP/USD moves lower, that means the GBP is losing value and the USD is gaining value. Duh, again, right?

The most important thing to remember is this: if you think the GBP is going to go up, then you buy GBP/USD. If you think the GBP is going to be weak, then you sell GBP/USD. How do you know if it is strong or weak? That's what the training is all about.

LOTS

1 lot = a certain dollar amount of currency that you want

to trade. On a standard (the bigger size for retail traders) trading account, 1 lot equals $100,000 worth of currency. 10 standard lots would equal $1,000,000 worth of currency. On a mini (smaller deposit required) account, 1 lot equals $10,000 worth of currency. 10 mini lots would equal $100,000 worth of currency, or in other words, 10 mini lots is equal to 1 standard lot. Got it?

PIP ME UP

A pip is the basic unit in a currency quote. If the GBP/USD is trading at 1.9112, then the "2" is the pip — it is the last number in the currency quote. If the price for the pair moves up to 1.9120, then the pair has moved up 8 pips. The value of each pip is dependent on how large your trade is. The table below shows approximate pip values for certain trade sizes.

Amount Traded	$ Per Pip
$10,000	$1
$100,000	$10
$500,000	$50
$1,000,000	$100
$5,000,000	$500

MARKET ORDER

This is when you tell your dealer, by pushing a button on your trading platform, or by calling the customer service number, to buy or sell a currency pair for you at the next available current price. If you trade using market orders, you won't always get the price that you see on your screen. You could get filled at a price higher or lower than what you saw on your screen.

ENTRY ORDER

This is when you tell your dealer, by pushing a button on your trading platform, or by calling the customer service number, to buy or sell a currency pair for you, at a specific price that you request. When the currency pair hits that price, then your trade will be executed whether you are awake, asleep, alive or dead. Most entry orders are guaranteed except directly after high-volatility economic reports. The guarantee means that you get the price you wanted – which is an advantage over market orders.

STOP LOSS ORDER

This is a price at which you want your dealer to automatically exit the trade if the trade moves against you. The name says it all — you are stopping your loss at a certain predetermined level. Let's say you buy the GBP/USD at 1.9000, and you are not willing to lose more than 50 pips. You can tell your dealer ahead of time (by a calling or using the software) to exit you automatically at 1.8950. You can set this order at the same time you open the trade with a market order. You can also set this parameter up at the same time you set up your entry order trade.

Stops are essential because they cap your losses at a set level. You can't be successful if you simply let your losses run forever.

LIMIT / TAKE PROFIT ORDER

This is a price at which you want your dealer to automatically exit the trade if the trade moves in your favor. Let's say you buy the GBP/USD at 1.9000, and you know that your profit goal on the trade is 50 pips. You can tell your dealer ahead of time (by a calling or using the software) to exit you automatically at 1.9050. You can set this order at the same time you open the trade with a market order. You can also set this parameter up at the same time you set up your entry order trade.

MARGIN

Buying and selling on margin means that you can control a large amount of currency (multiple lots) for a small initial investment.

For most retail trading accounts, dealers give you 100:1 margin. This means that if you "put up" $1,000 US, you can trade $100,000 US worth of currency.

Let's say you have $2,000 in your trading account. And you would like to place a trade to buy $10,000 (1 mini lot) of GBP/USD.

Your dealer deducts $100 from your account and you are left with a balance of $1,900. That remaining $1,900 that you have in your account balance is used to cover losses that you incur while trading.

If the trade goes against you, and you start to lose money, your trade will be closed with a "margin call" when your losses meet or exceed $1,900 (folks, at $1 per pip, you would have to let the trade go 1,900 pips against you before this trade closed with a margin call. If you let this happen, you are an idiot). When your trade is closed, the $100 that you "put up" for margin is now placed back into your account balance column, and you are left with that $100 for trading. Or for wiping the tears from your eyes for letting a trade go so long against you.

It's important that you remember what you just learned above, because every pip equals a certain dollar amount. Remember the table a few pages ago, that showed how much money a pip is worth, based on the size of the trade? When you trade $10,000, each pip equals $1. If you only have a $300 account, you have to trade very conservatively, so you don't end up blowing up your entire account on a losing trade.

This is why I suggest you trade with a reputable currency dealer that offers what is called "base 10" pricing. This means that your currency dealer allows you to set the value of a pip — you can even choose to trade small amounts of currency so that each pip equals as little as 10 cents. This means that you can open a small live account, and trade without feeling like you're going to lose everything. GFT offers this type of trading, as does OANDA (with more restrictive margin requirements). Dealers change their policies often, so your best bet is to check your dealer's website to see if they offer base 10 pricing.

Here are some dealers that do offer base 10:

http://www.gftforex.com
http://www.forex.com
http://www.oanda.com

Chapter Two

Strategy: 10

Strategy:10 was the first ebook I ever wrote. And it's still the most popular. I wrote it because I was worried that too many traders were trying to find too many 100-pip trades. You might have noticed this already, but in case you haven't, I'll repeat it: there are not many 100-pip trades just waiting for you.

When I realized that many traders were looking for huge wins, but ending up with huge losses, I decided to share something that helped me enormously when I first started out.

I simply looked for 10 pip trades. Getting in and out of the trade after 10 pips was a lot easier than looking for the big winner. It was less stressful. And I was able to find far more methods for grabbing 10 pips than I was for getting 100. Over time, I have altered the strategy to fit different market conditions and different currency pairs.

For example, it's no longer enough just to go for 10 pips and get out. The market is too volatile. What's better is if you go for 10 pips and then:

1. Sometimes move your stop to break even.
2. Some of the time get out with 10 pips.

If you do this when you are first starting out, you are going to get a good mix of 10 pip winners, 15-30 pip losers, break evens, and 20-100 pip winners. But where do you set your stop? How do you know when to take your profit?

I can hear the wheels spinning in your brain. So let's get down to business.

We'll start with a story:

A bear chased two hikers. One hiker, while being chased, stopped to put on running shoes. As he was changing out of his hiking boots, his companion looked at him in horror and exclaimed, "What in the world are you doing? You'll never outrun the bear if you stop now!"   Calmly, the other hiker said, "I don't have to outrun the bear. I just have to outrun you."

Currency trading can be like running away from the bear. Trading forex offers more opportunity for fast financial success – and financial ruin – than almost any other market. The get-rich crowd has always been attracted to it. This crowd includes speculators, trading novices, me 6 years ago, retirees, and professionals looking for a way to get out of debt, increase the excitement in their lives, or simply get rich really   fast.

Up until now, this group might have also included you.

From now on, you will be taking money away from these people. These are the people who will be eaten by the bear. You don't have to outrun the bear (the entire market). In fact, that's impossible. You can't beat the entire market. But you can trade defensively — and by so doing, position yourself to profit consistently.

But first we need to look at the four groups of currency traders, and find out which group you're in.

THE FOUR GROUPS

There are four types of participants in currency trading. There are the **novice traders** – the greenies, the ones who try to outrun the bear and lose every time. We all start here.

In addition to the novice traders, there are three other levels of participation: the **dealers**, the **institutional traders**, and the **advanced retail traders**.

In all of your trading, the **dealers** are the most powerful and they make the market, setting prices and putting together deals. Although institutional traders move more money around than dealers, it is still the case that your dealer either accepts or rejects your orders every time you trade.

The **institutional traders** work in banks, wire firms, or government agencies. They trade huge amounts of money at a time, and the size of their trades gives them enormous power. Some of these traders are moving $1 billion in currency or more every hour. Some are trading tens of billions of dollars every minute.

Next, there are the **advanced retail traders**. This group is comprised of people from all across the world, sitting in smaller investment firms, offices, or even their homes. Eventually, you want to be a part of this group. In some cases, the advanced traders are the smartest group – trade for trade – than any other group. Because they don't move a lot of money on each trade, they don't have as much power as the institutional players. Because their trades are brokered by the dealers, they'll never have absolute price-setting power. But, because there are so many novice traders, the advanced traders have plenty of people that they can outrun. Your goal as a currency trader is to aggressively take money out of the pockets of the novice traders.

Don't feel bad about that. Someone's going to take your money along the way, and it's going to teach you, very quickly, lessons that can only be learned through failure. So, every time you take money from a novice trader, just remember: you're teaching him a valuable lesson. After a while, you might even enjoy watching your hiking companion being eaten by the bear.

Well, you might not enjoy it. But you will deserve every pip you earn.

CAN YOU LIVE OFF OF 10 PIPS PER TRADE?

Remember our earlier discussion (see Chapter One) about the value of a pip? If you trade 1,000,000 worth of currency, each movement would be equal to $100. So if you bought at 1.1445 and sold at 1.1545, you would make 100 x $100, or $10,000. Now, I don't know about you, but I could live off of that much.

That's not saying, however, that you can make $10,000 per day. Of course it's possible, but there are a lot of factors that make it very difficult. Consider the questions below, that you might ask yourself before trading:

When should I get in a trade?
Where should I place my stop loss?
What happens if something goes wrong?

Even more importantly, can you deal with the emotions of forex trading? Alan Farley, a trading expert, rightly observes that mastering the emotions of trading is more difficult than mastering the technical skills. You'll soon find out what he means by that.

GREED

Most traders in the forex market try to make a zillion dollars on every trade.

They're greedy. This leads them to stay in a good trade, hoping to get more money out of it. This can lead to disaster — the trade can move against them and they get creamed. This happens all the time, and it still happens to me from time to time. It's the single greatest threat in trading. But you can already understand why that's probably true. But how do you overcome greed when trading?

REVENGE

This is the other big one. A lot of traders flush some pips down the toilet and then want to strike back. So they double their last order and go for broke. It's like, well ... it's like reaching down into your toilet. That's gross. And it does not make you any richer.

The impulse to get revenge is natural, and I still deal with this emotion often.

Do not underestimate this emotion. Many traders have not only reached into the toilet of revenge, but have dived into it head-first. Remember: the market is not your friend. The market is so much more powerful than you are. You cannot "get back at" the market. Trading when angry or vengeful will be a total disaster. If you take a big loss, then stop, take a deep breath, and talk to a mentor or your mirror, or your favorite stuffed animal. Re-read the charts. Take a break. Chew on your toe if you have to. Even if you think you see the best opportunity in the world after you get blasted – make sure you take a deep breath and pause before you do anything.

A DEFENSIVE APPROACH

It's as simple as this: When I am day trading, I don't try to make a ton of money on each trade, and I never try to get revenge.

Instead, I set up good trades, that have a lot of potential, and then I shoot for 10 pips as an initial target. Just 10 pips. That's it. I don't let myself lose a lot of money. I only try to get 10 pips at first, and if that's all I get, then I'm out for the day. We'll talk about how I try for more than 10 pips in a moment.

For now, consider that it's easy enough to get 10 pips

and, if that is all you can get, it's *okay* to get out. When you know that you can turn turn $10,000 into $130,000 in one year on 10 pips a day, it's no longer important to strike back at the market or get greedy on one day of trading.

And you can learn to turn $10,000 into $130,000 in one year on just 10 pips a day. I am not promising that you can do that. I am saying that it is possible and I have taught traders who have done it.

If you started with $10,000 on January 1st, and earned 10 pips per day, and only traded 17 days of the month, then you could end the year 2,000 pips UP, and with about $130,000. For a spreadsheet that details the progression in gains up to $130,000, write me at rob@robbooker.com, with the word "10 pip spreadsheet" in the subject line.

Why is this innovative, different, or revolutionary? Because you are going to not only take money from novices with this strategy, you're going to take money from other advanced traders. Advanced traders want big money. They didn't spend years learning to trade so that they could make $100 a day. They want big, big returns. They go for 40, 50, 100 pips at a minimum. Jimmy Young, an accomplished currency trader and a friend of mine, only trades a few times per month and goes for 100 pips or more every time. I also teach and take these types of trades myself. But it's only one way of approaching the market, and it's not easy.

Advanced traders are conservative with their trading capital because the market can take BIG swings against them when they're waiting for 100+ pips. Some advanced traders will think you're nuts for getting out of a trade at 10 pips. What if it goes to 100 pips? Or 200? Won't I be upset that I missed out?

Not at all. I'll show you later how I can still make 40, 50, or 100+ pips on these trades. But I'm never displeased with 10.

Let me repeat that:

I am never displeased with 10 pips of profit.

You should be grateful for any profit the market gives

you. Don't spend any time crying about how you didn't get the maximum profit, or how you could have gotten so much more profit if you just stayed in the trade longer. If you want to do anything about it, then stay in the damn trader longer next time. I'll tell you how you can do that.

GETTING MORE THAN 10 PIPS

Let's say that I find a great opportunity to go for 10 pips on a trade. I submit a market order, to buy the EUR/USD at 1.2900. I set a stop at 1.2880 (20 pips) and I do not set a limit order.

I am now long (because I bought) the EUR/USD at 1.2900.

When the price that I can sell at reaches 1.2910, I have earned 10 pips. I can either exit the trade with my profit, or stay in the trade longer. Here is how I stay in the trade:

I move my stop to break even. If my initial stop was 20 pips (or, on this trade, at 1.2880), then I move my stop to 1.2900. That means that if the price falls back to 1.2900 my trade automatically closes and I have lost nothing. I have gained nothing. I have traded defensively.

But if the trade goes to 1.2920, and 1.2930, and beyond, I am prepared to get more money. I can lose nothing — I am in a 100% risk free trade. Now I can let my profit run and I don't have to worry about anything.

Many traders ask me why I would do something like that. Why would I accept a break even trade? My answer is a question:

Out of 10 trades, would you accept 5 break even trades, 2 losers of 20 pips, and 2 winners of 50 each? I would. That's trading defensively, and it's what I want you to do.

How do you know when to just get out with 10 pips? I say, get out with 10 pips any time you want. It's ok to just take 10 pips.

How can you make money if your stop loss is at 20 or 30 pips and your gain is only 10 pips? You're not going to take 10 pips every time. This is not going to be your only trading strategy. This is one part of your trading toolbox. Other types of trades that you will take will get you more than 10. Lastly, remember that you are going to move your stop to break even sometimes and go for more than just 10 pips.

That said, I have taught traders who have learned to trade for 10 pips of profit more than 90% of the time.

They have made a lot of money going for small gains.

If you earned 10 pips every day for the next 12 months, and you started next year with over $100,000 in your trading account, you could be making between $10,000 and $17,000 per month trading (depending on your risk tolerance – remember, you can choose how many lots you trade). Can you do this? Absolutely. Can you do this today? Maybe, maybe not. You have to dedicate yourself 100% to learning how to trade intelligently.

HOW DO YOU FIND 10-PIP TRADES?

Here are seven principles of 10-pip trading:

Principle 1: Buy and sell on breakouts of support and resistance. Or, sell when a currency pair hits resistance and buy when it hits support. I teach this in the 1 on 1 training, and this is my major trading strategy.

Principle 2: Stop trying to make $8 million on every trade.

Principle 3: Set a 10-pip limit only. Exit the trade at 10. Exit the trade at 10. Stops are set based on market conditions, but are always set.

Principle 4: Goal: + 10 pips every time you trade. You don't have to trade every single day. Only trade when the market shows you an opportunity.

Principle 5: If I earn more than 10 pips on a trade because the trade moves so fast in my direction, I can set my stop to protect the 10 and then go for more.

Principle 6: There is no 'makeup' strategy. If I take a loss, then I'm just trying to end up with a 10 pip gain for the day. If I can't get it, then I don't try for 20 the next day, or whatever. I can keep trying for the 10 pips gain as long as I haven't lost more than 5% of my capital.

Principle 7: Time: I can trade for a set number of hours per day, meaning I can have the trading platforms open and sit at my computer for a max of, say, 5 hours per day. If I can't earn my 10 pips during that time, then I can set my stops and limits and walk away, but I can't actively watch the market any longer.

So, what kind of daily routine does it take to be a 10-pip trader? Here's one example.

Here's a daily routine that I've used in the Strategy:10 system. Some of the most successful months of my trading career happened when I followed this plan.

Up at 3:00 am Eastern Standard Time (when the market is most active). Check the charts.

Ask the following questions:

Where did the USD close (5pm EST) yesterday against the majors?

What effect will today's economic reports have, if any, on the forex market?

Are we at an all time high or low on any currency pair?

What one pair am I going to focus on today?

Where are the major areas of support and resistance on this pair?

What are some good breakout entries? Some good entries when a pair fails to break out?

Following this set of questions does not ensure that you are going to earn 10 pips every trade. But it certainly helps you. The most important question you can ask is **What is the major trend in the currency pair that I am watching?** If you trade with the trend, you are more likely to be able to find some 10 pip trading opportunities.

Stages of your trading career as described by actual Def Leppard song titles.

"Let Me Be the One"
"Promises"
"Rock Rock (Till You Drop)"
"Now"
"Unbelievable"
"Everyday"
"Pour Some Sugar On Me"
"Let's Get Rocked"
"Scar"
"It Don't Matter"
"Hysteria"
"Cry"
"Wasted"
"Bringin' On the Heartbreak"
"Four Letter Word"
"Disintegrate"

Chapter Three

The Role of Confidence

"I can't beat him. But that don't bother me. The only thing I want to do is to go the distance, that's all. Because if that bell rings and I'm still standing, then I'm gonna know for the first time in my life, see, that I wasn't just another bum from the neighborhood."

- Rocky Balboa, Rocky I

In trading, confidence is essential. Arrogance is fatal.

Okay, so Rocky Balboa never existed. But he was my hero as a kid and it never mattered to me that it was just a movie. He was the consummate street fighter, faced with impossible odds (even before he was invited to fight Apollo Creed) just to eek out an existence in urban Philadelphia.

You have to know right now, from the very beginning, that you can't beat the market. Admit that the market is bigger, stronger, badder than you are. The market is the current heavyweight champion of the world, and you're nuts if you think that you can register a TKO in any round. In any trade. I believe that the single greatest downfall of the average trader is too much pride. Going for too many pips. Arrogance bred of the last trade.

By now, you've learned that the market doesn't give a damn about you, about your need to support your family, or about your last winning trade that was the best, most amazing, most coolest thing ever done by a forex trader.

The market wants that money back. There are thousands of traders out there who lost yesterday, and the market does not care about any of them.

But the trick is that you don't have to beat the market.

And all you have to do is go the distance. You just have to survive long enough to land some great punches.

THE TWO ATTITUDES

It's generally accepted in the world today that people that believe in a positive attitude and "the power of positive thinking" are out of their freaking minds. I can understand that. When I read Norman Vincent Peale's groundbreaking book, I sort of felt like I was stepping back into the 1950's. Like I was sitting inside a Norman Rockwell painting. I didn't feel comfortable there, and I can understand that positive thinking has sort of gone out of style.

But it's going to be one of the most important advantages as you trade.

Your attitude determines, in large part, whether you are going to chose to protect your account or if you are going to play cowboy. It either points the way to profits or losses.

The two attitudes that we're going to discuss in this chapter are arrogance and Confidence.

ARROGANCE

Arrogance is the outward display of your confidence, with a twist of pride.

It's the belief that you are bigger than the market. That you're bigger than the next big thing. That every trade you make is a winner, and that you can do no wrong. Have you ever met a trader who bragged about his system until you felt like punching him?

Remember when Apollo Creed agreed to fight Rocky? He didn't so much as consider for one moment that he, the heavyweight champion of the world, could lose. He called Rocky a chump. Looking beyond the fight, he just knew he was going to win, and that no one could beat him. The whole fight was just a promotion for his fame.

If you think of the market in the same way, you're going to get creamed. You're going to stop protecting yourself. You've seen this type of trader, or at least heard about him. He's the guy that brags to you that he averages 300 pips a month. But he isn't bragging when he takes a 1,000 pip hit over a 5 day period. He rarely admits to losses. In fact, he keeps his weaknesses private and refuses to discuss them.

He trades on demo after demo, reaching profitability, then suffering seemingly insurmountable losses, so he simply starts over with a new demo, all the while taking his best days, weeks, and months, and patching them together to claim that he's becoming the Master of Disaster, the King of Sting. *This is not a way to build confidence. By starting off as arrogant, he ends up totally without any confidence at all.*

The reason that this attitude is so dangerous is that it encourages the following behaviors:

1. Getting into trades based on emotion.
2. Staying in horrible trades even after realizing the mistake.
3. Making too many trades in a one day.

In all of the above examples, you're eventually going to give all of your profits back to the market, to the real heavyweight champion.

THE ROLE OF CONFIDENCE

For the purposes of trading, confidence has the following definition:

A humble, calm attitude that leads a trader to determine that he will patiently acquire and retain profits.

When you take on an attitude of confidence, you set yourself up to win. You believe that the market is bigger than you, that it's not going to go down in the first round – but if you stay with it, you're going to at least get some great punches in. When you're confident, you believe that there is a respectable amount of profit available to you on every trade, and that you simply have to wait for the opportunity to come to you.

Plan on going the distance against the market. This means that you're willing to spend some time in front of the computer. That you're willing to keep a trading journal, even though it requires time and effort. That you visit the local bookstore or library and read everything you can about technical and fundamental analysis. That you wake up early. That you learn to acquire more discipline. That once you enter a trade, you're willing to go the distance with it, but (unlike Rocky) you're not willing to bleed to death just to prove a point.

When you have confidence, the following things happen:

A confident trader never does anything that would risk losing more than 10% of his account. It's ok to lose on a trade. It is never ok to lose more than 5%-10% of your account on a single trade or set of trades that are open simultaneously. Ever.

Decide right now that you are never going to do anything to risk losing a substantial amount of your account. Period. There is no excuse for this. Your trading account is precious. It represents the amount of money that will bring you financial freedom. Never risk losing it. It is not money to be spent "learning how to trade." Never risk real money on stupid trades. If you ever do anything to lose your entire account, from this time forward, you are just an idiot. You have no excuse for it. It upsets me that many people that I have met have lost a substantial amount of their trading capital right as they figure out how to trade profitably. A confident trader saves his account for the time when he will know best what trades to take.

A confident trader never trades on emotion. You just know when to trade and when not to trade. Impulse trades will kill you. If you find that you are sitting down a the computer, and you are about to take a trade only because the market is moving and you do not want to miss the move, then you MUST walk away. This is when you need to shut off the computer. A confident trader doesn't need a quick fix just to try to score some fast gains. A confident trader understands that an impulse trade is like lowering his hands in a boxing match – he is going to get punched in the face. When you take an impulse trade, you have no plan. And when you have no plan, but a trade is open, it's nearly impossible to objectively figure out what you need to do next. Decide right now that you are never again going to open an impulse trade, period. Decide now that if you do open an impulse trade that you:

1. Will do 100 push ups, unless you are medically unable.
2. Will do 100 practice trades on historical charts before you trade again.

A confident trader never brags about his abilities. This is the precursor to becoming arrogant. It's ok to make jokes about how you are going to bully the market into submission. It's ok to tell yourself that you are going to do better next week than you did this week. But it is much more important to buckle down and do your planning and homework so that you are actually ready to do better next week. Most traders say that they are going to do better, but then they go watch "CSI" or "Desperate Houswives" or "Press Your Luck."

A confident trader pulls the trigger on the trades she plans. Make the decision now that every day you are going to set aside time for trade planning. I do this every evening, for at least two hours, between 3pm and 12 midnight Eastern Time. You have to plan first. Even if you are a short term trader, using the 5 or 15 minute charts, you need to make sure that you make a division between your planning time and your trading time.

I have found that some of the best traders I have ever worked with struggle with pulling the trigger, with taking their own trades. This is hard for anyone who wants to protect their account. But here is the key: get yourself a trading partner, and announce to that person the trades you are going to take. This person will hold you to your plans. Your trading partner will be there to ask you if you followed through on your plans to trade. If you did not follow through on your plans to trade, we go back to square one:

If you do not follow through on your plan to trade a setup, then you must go back in time on historical charts, and trade forward candle by candle, for at least 25 trades.

A confident trader practices trading. What I just described above is called "manual backtesting" and it is one of the best confidence boosters you can do. By playing candles forward one at a time, you are showing yourself that you know how to trade. You are practicing without risking any real money. If you are not doing this right now, then start. If your charting platform does not allow you to play candles forward one at a time, then you need to switch to a new charting package. You need to do at least 50 practice trades per week. Keep a notebook with the results.

A confident trader understands her relationship with money. What do most people do if they find € 20 on the street in Paris? They spend it. Often people treat "found money" as if it were meaningless. My mother used to tell me that money must be burning a hole in my pocket, because I wanted to spend it so fast. Unless you solve your relationship problems with money first, you are not going to be a confident trader.

You have to learn to be an accumulater of money. This means that your goal is to amass a huge pile of money in your regular bank account, not just your trading account. It means that when you have a profitable trade, that you set some of that money aside. It means that every time your trading account grows, you raise the high watermark on your account and do not allow yourself to lose what you have gained.

A confident trader never believes that she has figured out the market. This is a nice way to lose your life's savings.

Names for Forex Dealers that Would Never Work.

Pip Thieves

We're Cooking the Books and Are About to Go BankruptFX

Fat Louie's BBQ and Forex

Chapter Four

Mr. Spock on Trading

Do you remember Spock from the television series *Star Trek?*
I do. I remember him because he was always so calm and
collected. This guy never seemed to get frazzled. Nothing
bothered him. You could cut out his heart and he would say
something like, "That is no logical," whereas most of us
would say, "Stop cutting out my heart."
After all, this was the guy who said:

> "Emotions are alien to me. I'm a scientist."
> -- Spock, "This Side of Paradise", stardate 3417.3

Of course, Spock would make a great trader, would he
not? He would be able to take a 500 standard lot trade and
sit back and calmly evaluate his options, and have a slice of
Targ or Bark or whatever it was that Vulcans ate.

It seems that there is a myth that has been heavily promoted throughout the world of trading – the myth that successful traders lack emotion.

This is a load of crap. Emotions are central to successful trading. Spock will show us why.

LESSON 1: USE YOUR FEAR

Don't do that anymore!   You need to wake up and instead of going straight to the computer, try some of the following things to help you get into the right frame of mind:

1. **Meditate or pray.**
2. **Read your trading plan (you do have one, right?)**
3. ~~**Call your mother**~~
4. **Eat a piece of fruit**
5. **Read a chapter from a book on trading**

Or, sit and quietly think about a trade that went very well, something recent, and picture in your mind doing that again.

When you have done that, make sure that you spend time getting familiar with where the market is. Are trades that you planned the night before ready to execute? What if the trades have opened already?

Consider following only one currency pair, especially early on in your career as a trader. If you work full time this is even more important. You can't follow 5 pairs every day. You don't need to and it's not productive. When you focus on one currency pair, and you learn everything there is to know about that pair, you reduce the anxiety associated with trading.

Most of us are frightened by what we don't understand (trading is full of surprises, too). You can reduce your fear substantially by becoming so familiar with a currency pair that you understand how it moves, when it moves, what economic reports move it most, what moving averages work with it best, and so on.

Don't skimp on the time that you give yourself to get familiar with a currency pair.

Consider the following situation: you wake up to an alarm that goes off when a trade you planned the night before is trigged.   What do you do?   Generally, you rush to the computer and you start trading.

But let's slow things down a bit. Even if the trades you have prepared the night before have already opened, please take just 30 seconds and prepare yourself mentally. Sit quietly for a moment. Take a deep breath. Picture in your mind how you will react to seeing a profitable trade, or a losing trade.   Imagine yourself handling the trade with poise and confidence, just like Spock would expect you to do.

Then open up your trading software and panic. You are going to anyway, right?

LESSON 2: CHANNEL YOUR ANGER

Have you ever been angry after a trading mistake?   That's good. We can use that to your advantage.

"Where there's no emotion, there's no motive for violence."
-- Spock, "Dagger of the Mind", stardate 2715.1

What, no violence?   Trading gives us plenty of motives for violence!

Please get angry when you make a stupid mistake. If you violate your trading rules, get angry. Get angry if you plan to get out with 25 pips of profit and then, for whatever reason, you let the trade go (thinking you can get more) and you then lose 25 instead of making 25. That is not excusable.

Even get angry at a loss. Yes, that's right – go ahead and get as angry as you want. Stomp around. Yell some. Grit your teeth. You should not be happy about losses, and there is no point to saying, "Oh, well, losing is part of the game, and I need to lose in order to learn. In fact, when I lose, I learn a lot."

Bull crap.

Go ahead and get angry. But here's the key: Channel that anger into applying yourself more aggressively to learning how to trade. Ask yourself how you can do better. Write down what you did right in the trade, and what you did wrong. Talk to your trading partner, coach, team member, or dog. Discuss what you need to do to improve NOW.

Losers excuse their losses as learning opportunities. It's okay to say that you learned from your mistakes. But losers keep making mistakes and then saying that they are learning. That is stupid.

Make better trades. Learn from your profitable trades.

Stop excusing yourself when you do something stupid in a trade.

Take responsibility.

The problem for nearly every beginning trader I have ever known is not that they *have* emotions (that would be an unsolvable problem). The problem is that most traders succumb to high emotion, and then they toss their trading plan into the toilet and start making terrible trades. You have to use your emotions to boost your dedication to creating and following a profitable trading plan.

LESSON 3: DON'T TRADE ALONE

You should trade with a team. Trading with a team – whether it's one person or 5, can help you.

> "No one can guarantee the actions of another."
> -- Spock, "Day of the Dove", stardate unknown

We'll, there's another worthless quote from Spock. What the hell is he talking about? I think that trading in a team can help you make sure that you use your emotions properly. When I trade in a team, the others keep me grounded and as stable as possible. I get angry, and they help me channel my anger.

I get cautious after a loss, and they help me plan my way through that emotion.

When you trade as a team, or plan trades as a team, you are accountable to live up to what you promised. If you say you are going to exit at 25 pips, and you don't, then you have to face the team. If you say you are done trading for the day, and you take more trades, then you are going to have to explain yourself to the team.

As part of my 1 on 1 training, I set forex traders up into teams – and they find that they are able to focus less on the emotions of trading and more on making good trades. In fact, working with a team has enabled some traders to completely avoid some of their biggest emotional weaknesses.

LESSON 4: GREED KILLS

Greed will kill you. It will destroy your profits.

"Dude, why did you keep trading? That is not logical, especially when you were up 50 pips. "
-- Spock, "Bad Spike", stardate unknown

Greed will tempt you to make a deadly mistake: overtrade.

Many traders keep trading because they are addicted. Many keep trading because they want to get revenge on the market. The only good reason to keep trading is because you see that there is an opportunity to make more money. Never trade because you are in the mood to trade.

If you want to have a good time and don't care about your money, just light your Euros or Pounds or Yen on fire and have a weenie (hot dog) roast. That is much more fun, you can invite friends over, and at the end of the day you will have more to show for it. And you might even save some money.

How do you know the difference between taking lots of good trades and overtrading? In other words, how do you know when you are on a roll vs. getting yourself set up for disaster? Or how do you know when a winning trade is coming soon even after a few losses?

I ask myself a few simple questions:

Am I following my tested trading plan? If not, how can I have a reasonable expectation of success? Unless I am testing a new system on a demo account, why would I trade outside of my plan?

How many trades have I taken today? If it's more than I usually take, then why do I need to take another one?

What's the expected gain or loss from this next trade? I strongly encourage you to consider every trade from the standpoint of how much you stand to lose if the trade goes all the way to your stop loss. Too often, traders focus on what they can gain, not what they can lose. And guess what? By focusing on how much they can gain, they make stupid mistakes. They start buying big screen TVs and cars and mortgage payments with the gains that they don't even have.

The most important questions there are in #1. Let the market tell you to trade. If your trading system is tested, and the market shows a trade signal, then take the trade. Period. If you are considering a trade outside your plan, then stop yourself and get away from the computer.

Consider also the number of trades you're taking. Many traders start overtrading and never stop to realize it. Stop every morning or evening while you're trading and simple add up the number of trades you took – is it way above average? That is probably not a good sign.

Chapter Five

The Woodchuck and the Possum

A friend of mine volunteers on a regular basis to rid his neighborhood of rodents and animal riff-raff: the woodchucks, groundhogs, and possums that eat up gardens, attack family pets, and so on. He sets a trap with ripe fruit or tuna fish. The animal enters the trap for the food. If the animal can't find its way out, it is eventually shot and buried.

In the currency trading, sometimes you get the fruit.
Sometimes you get trapped and shot. Why?

Possums are relatively easy to catch. They go for the fruit, they get caught, and then, when the trapper approaches the trap, the possum simply plays dead. It plays dead because that's the best defense mechanism that it has.

A woodchuck is tougher to trap. A big one might enter the trap, eat the fruit, and then rip the trap apart, exit, and wander off looking for more food. Or it might roll the trap along the ground, set it off, and then eat the fruit from the outside.

There is a fundamental characteristic of unsuccessful currency traders: they trade forex because it's exciting, cool, or for its sex appeal. The mystery behind the charts, the notion that profits (although elusive) do really exist, and that money can be made quickly (but not predictably) all add up to create a romantic fantasy that is too appealing to avoid. When they start to lose money, they leave their positions open, close their eyes, and hope that the trap is miraculously opened so they can be free again.

This group – the Possums – is the largest block of forex traders.

There is also a fundamental characteristic of successful forex traders. They trade forex because it makes them rich. They trade because they know how to do it. They do not trade for fun. Many of them are unimpressed by their own success.

Most of them never share their secrets with anyone. They take a methodical, almost boring, approach to forex trading. They painstakingly build systems that, although simple, may have taken years to perfect. In the end, their lives are actually quite boring – reduced to waiting for predictable signals that are obeyed without question.

This group – the Woodchucks – is the smaller of the two groups. The Possums outnumber the Woodchucks by a ratio of at least 500:1. For every Woodchuck, there are 500 Possums.

Are you a Woodchuck or a Possum?

Possums don't want to learn the intricacies of the forex market – the charts, the signals, the nuts and bolts – because they are afraid that once known, all these details will ruin the romanticism of the entire adventure. The mystery, the elusive profits, the unknown, all contribute to create an excitement that would be lost if too much were discovered. Searching for King Tut or the Titanic was big news. Finding both was big news. When's the last time you heard about either? Once found, the mystery was solved and the public went on to other mysteries.

Woodchucks want to learn the market. They want to know what signals are most predictive. They want to know everything they can not only about spot trading, but about their broker, their broker's practices, the governments involved in currency movement, interest rate changes, and the list goes on and on. Woodchucks want to know as much as they can. It might destroy the mystery, but they're not in the forex market for adventure. They're in it for profit.

There is a myth in American culture, and it's spreading around the world: your job should be fun. You should enjoy what you do for a living. "Do what you love and the money will follow." And so on. Perhaps we've had too strong of a dose of this doctrine. The truth is that although we are better off choosing a career that interests us, we're going to be bored at work if we learn our job really well. The promise is simple: if you become a world-class forex trader, at some point your job will be ho-hum. Not all the time, but it's not going to be an adventure every day of the week. Sorry.

On the other hand, consider that successful forex traders are some of the most highly paid professionals **in the world**. If you pay them by the hour, they make thousands and thousands of dollars for every 60 minute period they spend working. Some of them only trade for a half day. Some trade for 20 hours a day. Their jobs aren't always fun, but they do make a lot of money.

WHY BE A WOODCHUCK?

Simply put, if you want to survive, then you need to start thinking like a Woodchuck. If you want to make money, you need to commit yourself to freeing yourself from the trap *and* getting the fruit. Or, more importantly, finding a way to eat the fruit without ever entering the trap in the first place. And therein lies the secret. We're all going to get trapped from time to time, but we have a choice of whether to free ourselves or lay down and let the trapper shoot us.

I learned my lesson early in my career as a currency trader. Although I had spent four months creating a trading strategy and system, I occasionally *really, really* wanted the fruit, so to speak. At those times, when I should have stayed on the sidelines of the market, I would enter trades based on rumor, speculation, or even well-informed opinions – instead of my tried and tested strategy. In other words, I would enter the trap and start eating the fruit, thinking that I could get out of the trap without setting it off.

Well, the last time I made this mistake, I entered a trade that lost 250 pips in 72 hours. I stayed in the trade hoping that the market would rebound (it never did). I figured if I just laid down quietly, the trapper would never come and shoot me. Well, he did. I lost my usable margin on the last day. I lost 75% of my account.

I resolved on that day to never again violate the principles of my trading strategy.

I tell everyone that trades forex the same thing: you can learn this the hard way, or the easy way. But you will learn it eventually: in the world of forex trading, there are only Woodchucks and Possums. If you're just trading on emotion, speculation, or excitement, then you're a Possum, and you're going to get shot. Either take it from me, or learn on your own. I hope you take the time to read the principles below and learn from my mistakes.

HOW TO BE A WOODCHUCK

There are five steps to thinking like a Woodchuck in the forex market.

Be hungry and determined. The Woodchuck wants the fruit. He believes that he has a right to it. He is willing to do whatever it takes to safely get it and eat it.

As for you, you've got to want profits. You've got to put profits ahead of everything else. You've got to say to yourself that the most important thing at the end of the money is not making lots of trades, or any trades, but rather the most important thing is to end the money higher than when you started it. This belief has to drive you. If you trade because you like to trade, you're going to lose money – you will end up making stupid trades, getting trapped, and laying down to wait for the bullet.

The Woodchuck wants to fill his belly – but not at the expense of his life. Remember that.

Be hungry for profits, not just for trades.

Discover true principles. The Woodchuck, unlike the Possum, can learn from its own mistakes or the mistakes of other animals. It understands that if it enters the trap, it will be caught. It knocks over the cage, sets it off, and then jumps back. When it senses the danger has passed, it might start poking at the cage from the outside, or try to grab the fruit through the bars of the cage.

Likewise, you need to become a student of the forex market if you want to become successful. The forex market does not reward lazy people. Plan on spending some money on books to become familiar with charting patterns. Read everything you can online about how the market works. Get some charting software – there is plenty of good free charting software to start you out – and watch the formations. Most important, start trading on a demo account immediately. Get involved, take notes. Keep a trading journal that lists every trade and the reason you entered and exited.

As you do these things, you will distill principles of the forex market. From the jumbled mess of data, patterns will emerge. Effective trading strategies will become apparent. Profits will still be elusive, but you will begin to learn true principles of trading. Write these principles down as you learn them. They will serve you well later.

Obey true principles. Once you discover a set of true principles, they'll do you no good if you disregard them. I've met forex traders that understood many, many true principles, but they were still dumb as a bag of hammers and poor as church mice because they failed to obey them.

Our culture isn't much fascinated with obedience – if you've noticed, we're all about how free we are, how unrestricted our behavior can and should be, and so on. This booklet isn't a commentary on social issues, but I do want to advise you that sticking to your principles may seem odd at first.

You might determine that although important, your principles are more "guidelines" than hard and fast rules. Don't fall for that! Don't spend all your time discovering true principles just so that you can violate them – and lose a lot of money in the process.

Once you discover what works, stick to the plan!

Mark Twain said that once he learned all of the intricacies involved in navigating the Mississippi – the steering of the boat, the reading of the compass, the charting of the deep and shallow points – that the river lost its beauty.

That's a lesson, a truth, that you're going to have to become comfortable with. At some point, when you develop a profitable trading system, the system will return profits if you're awake, asleep, playing football with your kids, or if you get hit by a bus. The system will be tweaked from time to time, of course, but it will work. Your hard work will pay off. But the mystery of the forex market will disappear for a time, maybe even forever, and thus your fascination with it might wear off too.

This is why many forex traders, although they have learned true principles, are still losing money as fast as they can trade. They want to chase the mystery of the market. They enter the cage to get the fruit because that's more exciting. It's also more dangerous. Even fatal.

Know your limits. One mistake Possums make is that they never set limits. They'll waltz into the cage and go for the fruit with reckless abandon. You might attribute this to stupidity, and you may be right. But it also might be due to their over-exuberance. Their inability to contain their excitement over finding some fruit.

You will be tempted to snatch the fruit as soon as you can see it. You might be tempted to violate your principles when you see the market take a big swing, or after Alan Greenspan says something on television, or the latest job report comes out. Sometimes, you'll be tempted to set your stop-loss very widely (thus risking the loss of a lot of money) or to not set a stop-loss at all.

In order to succeed, you must set stops. You have to be able to tell yourself that it's time to get out of the market, that you've tried to get the fruit – but that today it's just not going to work. Perhaps your system works 80% of the time, and this time your system has simply failed.

Getting out of the market at the right time is just as important as getting in at the right time. If your system tends to return 20 pips per trade, then set your stop-loss so that you don't lose more than you can possibly gain.

If you disobey your principles, and you find that you're in a big, big losing trade, then look at your trading system: do you really see the market coming back to break-even anytime soon? If not, then get out. If so, then stay in – if you have the usable margin to withstand some heavy losses.

Which brings me to my next point: don't trade huge chunks of your account. If you have a $1,000 account, then don't make trades that require you to put up more than $100. Also, don't make trades that can lose or gain more than $3 per pip. If the market takes a real nosedive against you, you could halve your equity before you realize what you've done.

Back off when necessary. When you lose a lot of money in one day, or gain a lot of money in one day, back off from the market. These are dangerous times. I talk about Pride, Fear, Greed, and Revenge in my Strategy:10 booklet (free, on my site) but it will help to summarize the main points here too.

Pride is your worst enemy. There is no such thing as "good pride" in the forex market. As soon as you become proud of your success, you're headed for a fall. When you're prideful, you leave yourself open to Greed and Revenge. You feel that you deserve more profit, are willing to take more (unwise) risks, and you strike back at the market when it beats you. Being prideful in the forex market is acting the same as the Possum who believes he can go into the cage, get the fruit, and still get out. It won't work. Keep your pride in check.

Next, watch out for Fear. When you're afraid, you make poor choices – you'll exit a trade before it becomes profitable or you'll enter no trades at all. If you give in to fear, then back off the market. Backtest your system again. Review what made you successful in the past. Take a day off and reset your bearings. You'll feel better and be ready to trade the next day.

Greed is perhaps the second worst emotion you can ever feel in the forex market. This emotion will convince you to set higher limits and wider stops, leaving you exposed to the wild swings of the market. Greed is what convinces you to leave a position open for one more pip of profit – when the market is about to slide in the opposite direction and take your entire profit with it. Don't give into greed. If you lose a bunch of money because of greed – or make a bunch of it – then take the next day off. Watch the market. Demo trade for that day. See how you fare. Then get back in the next day when you're ready to stick to your principles.

Revenge is the most dangerous emotion of all. When you lose money, you will always feel the temptation to strike back at the market (out of pride). You'll say to yourself that you deserve to get your money back. This might even work temporarily. But this will catch up with you, as you seek out trades for the sake of trading rather than for the sake of making money safely. If you feel revenge coming on, get out of the market. Take a seat. Review your system. Even if you lose almost all of your money, you can gain it back systematically. You will never get it back by seeking revenge on the market. A Possum in a cage might seek revenge against the trapper, but we all know how futile that is.

Chapter Six

The Miracle of Discipline

Have you ever exited a trade at a loss, only to find that the trade would have been profitable only a little while later?[1]

Have you ever exited a losing trade, opened one in the opposite direction, and then lost twice?

I have. I used to make those mistakes and many others.

Have you ever not stayed in a trade long enough to get the full amount of profit from it?

Discipline is the answer. Disciplined traders succeed and undisciplined traders fail. It's really that easy.

This isn't a chapter about currency trading, though – at least not directly. It's really about how you can learn to acquire greater discipline in your life, which will make you a better trader (*much* better). In fact, I promise that this book

---

[1] There is a longer version of this chapter available at the following internet address:

http://www.robbooker.com/Miracle_of_Discipline.pdf

will make you a better trader, as long as you're willing to give some of my advice a try. Once you've acquired greater discipline in your life, I've got a bunch of forex trading strategies that you can use (or you can find many, many others elsewhere). But none of those strategies are worth anything without discipline, because…

The problem with most trading systems is that they assume you already possess the discipline to implement them.

I have read just about every trading strategy book out there – and hundreds of self-help books -- and all of them have impacted my life positively. I'm a better trader for having read them. However, for much of my life I struggled with a lack of discipline, and as long as I struggled with discipline, I was always *almost* successful at whatever I tried. In the end, I was left with mountains of good advice and without the discipline to implement all of it consistently. After hundreds and hundreds of conversations with traders and successful people across the world, I realized that I wasn't alone, and for many people, the only obstacle blocking the path to trading profits (and other important accomplishments) is a lack of discipline.

My successes and my failures can be traced to the presence – or absence – of one human quality: discipline.

Having perfect discipline – not perfect strategy – is the key.

This book is about how to become a renown trader. Not just a good trader. But one of the very best. Not just a few thousand dollars per month. I want you to be a millionaire from your trading profits. In order to help you, I want you to understand that discipline is more important than, and it comes before, strategy. It's above tactics. Your *Discipline Quotient* – the level of your personal commitment to self-discipline – determines your trading profits. It is the single greatest factor in whether you become successful as a trader. I know that is a terribly presumptuous thing to say. I know you're thinking that I must be out of my mind. I promise you that I'm:

a. Not lying to you.
b. Have nothing to gain by lying to you.

I have freely distributed thousands of copies of this chapter in several editions, hoping that as many people will read it and comment on it (you can get a free ebook version of the book at http://www.robbooker.com). If I wanted to expose myself to ridicule, I could have done it in a much easier way by dropping my pants in the supermarket. I can't make any money from you unless you want to buy trading signals or training from me, which doesn't cost you very much anyway. Every dime I make on any copy of this edition of this book (and I don't make much more than a dime) is donated to charity.

My own journey to raise my Discipline Quotient is not complete. As I wrote this book, I was reminded of Robert Pirsig's insightful comment at the introduction of his book, *Zen and the Art of Motorcycle Maintenance*: that the book wasn't very accurate as far as fixing motorcycles was concerned, but the repairs to his bike were really just metaphors, anyway. I feel like I've written a book about discipline not because I was born with it, but rather because I've spent my life trying to gain more of it. Today, I trade for a living because I gained enough discipline to become successful.

Lastly, before you dive into this book, I want to encourage you to do a few things: write in the margins of this book. Take notes. Think this stuff through. Send copies to close friends and ask them to discuss it with you. I don't care how many times you copy this book and send it to friends as long as you don't change the writing *inside* of the margins or claim that you wrote it.

Email me at: rob@robbooker.com. I always answer every email that I receive. It might take me a few days, but I will respond.

Please let me know about your journey to become more disciplined.

PART 1: DISCIPLINE IS THE GREAT SEPARATOR

Discipline is what separates human accomplishment from human failure. It is what distinguishes bad from good. It is the Grand Canyon separating good from Great. Superior performance from mediocre accomplishment. A+ from C-. 10 points up from 100 points down. Discipline breathes life into every aspect of life; the lack of discipline sucks energy from all endeavors, characteristics, qualities, attributes, projects, goals, and people. Life can be led without discipline but it cannot be led well. This isn't something I believe because it sounds good. It's something I believe because I've lived with discipline and without discipline; I've talked to hundreds (maybe thousands) of people who have done the same; in every case, the disciplined life was the happier life.

For a long time, I felt like a failure. I would try new trading strategies, new ways of thinking, new goals, new relationships – but I would never be satisfied. During this time of my life I **wanted** to improve. For every goal, I didn't lack desire. But things seemed to stall after a while. I lost interest in the goals, the commitments, plans, or relationships. By moving to the next project, I would re-energize myself temporarily.

Repeatedly, I'd set a trading goal (sometimes the same one) and then lose steam somewhere along the way. Or I'd begin a book and then fail to complete it. Or, I'd start a relationship and blow it because I wasn't disciplined enough to love unselfishly. Worst of all, I'd enter a trade, set my stops and limits, then completely forget about those stops and limits. I lost a lot of money that way. I was gambling with my trades, my relationships, and my life.

Inevitably, I'd start over, promise myself I wouldn't do the same thing again....

Life became for me a series of *next* followed by *next*. Most of the time, I didn't consciously move from one to the other; I usually skipped to the next project with the rationale that I had *finally found* what I was meant to do. With each *next*, I brought back the spark of life that I had missed. However, each *next* brought a smaller and less enduring amount of passion.

This process eventually became unbearable.

It became unbearable because I lacked the discipline to finish what I started.

Someone once said that the definition of insanity is doing the same thing over and over and expecting a different result. As far as I'm concerned, the person who sad that was an idiot. Once I ate 14 scoops of ice cream in one sitting, but that didn't mean that I shouldn't eat ice cream any longer.[2] It is *perfectly* okay for you to set the same goal over and over, as long as it's the right goal for you and you care deeply about succeeding. My life is proof that you can try things more than once (like relationships) and expect success every time, regardless and in spite of past failures. The problem with the search for discipline is that most of us are afraid to keep trying the same thing over and over – we quit too quickly, and therefore we proclaim ourselves sane because we accepted the apparent futility of our actions. Well, discipline is all about not giving up, and trying the same (right) thing over and over until you get it right.

---

[2] This happened on the day I "graduated" from 7th grade. My friends and I walked to the ice cream parlor, where I really did eat the 14-scoop Volcano. This was a disciplined success that I still treasure to this day. It led to severe intestinal problems, but I always remind myself that every great accomplishment has its price.

I really believe that you and I cannot be exceptionally happy without discipline, in the same way that we cannot be exceptionally organized, wealthy, persuasive, or intelligent. We can be mediocre at *anything* without discipline (I have proven this time and time again). We can get through life just fine. We can be loved. We can enjoy our work. We can have a pleasant family life. If mid-level jobs, mid-level wealth, and mid-level happiness are acceptable to us, then acquiring discipline might not be worth the effort.

But I suspect that you're reading this book (and I wrote it) because we're unsatisfied with mediocrity. You're the kind of person who feels like they want more out of life and you're willing to improve any way possible. As far as the rest of the people out there – those who don't care if they improve – well, they're in good company! The nightclub of mediocrity is a great place to meet people. The majority of all humans unconsciously – or consciously – choose mediocrity. For a long time, I was a part of that mediocre majority.

Think quickly: who is the greatest person you have ever known? You can't answer that question and tell me that the person was mediocre. I'm not saying that the person was famous, or that the person didn't have any problems. I'm saying that you are impressed by that person because they were *more* than *ordinary*. And, more importantly, this person was extraordinary because they were – consciously or not – a disciplined person.

When I think of one of the greatest people I've known, I think of my aunt. She never played professional sports, ran a company, or appeared on television. She wasn't famous or rich. She was a psychotherapist in New York City. So, if she lacked fame and fortune, what made her great?

My aunt wrote her PhD dissertation on successful techniques of providing counseling to people with full-blown AIDS. These people had years to live (at most) and months to live (at worst). She counseled with these people. She helped them work through some of life's most painful issues: regret, sorrow, physical pain, and death. Most of her patients died before she completed her dissertation. I can't imagine the discipline that it required for her to finish this labor of love even as her patients passed away.

Without expectation of reward, she served these people selflessly and without judging them.

Here's an exercise for you:

Quick! Think of that great person again. A person who has influenced your life for the better. Write in the blanks below why that person affected your life. Say more about that person:

_____

_____

_____

_____

_____

_____

Now that you've taken the time to think about this person's story, ask yourself a question: How many influential people, like the one above, do you know? Probably only one or two. Or very few. When I just wrote this question, I instantly thought of my aunt again, who worked with over 200 dying people in the late 1980's, comforting them, counseling them, without compensation. I have known very few people as unselfish as she.

She could have completed a dissertation of lesser importance. One that perhaps required fewer sorrowing experiences. But she made a choice to do something that her heart told her to do, and she disciplined herself to complete the research.

By refusing to accept the status quo, my aunt forever claimed a place in her nephew's life, and in the lives of those she served. Likewise, if **you** choose to reject mediocrity and settle only for superior performance from yourself, then you are putting yourself on the fringes of society. You are willing to do what your heart tells **you** to do, despite obstacles, sorrow, fear, distraction – all those things that would prevent us from succeeding.   In a sense, you are willing to stand alone.   Near the end of her research, as my aunt cried (and typed a bit of her dissertation), and then cried some more, she felt as alone as she had ever felt ... nearly every patient she had treated was dead.

To summarize, here's the paradox: Even though discipline is the great separator – and sets us apart from those who accept mediocrity, you'll also find that as you follow your heart with discipline, others will be attracted to you. You will influence the lives of others for good. You will be an example to those around you of the fact that all of us, no matter what, have a calling, and that you have the power to succeed.

PART 2: DISCIPLINE IS THE GREAT LEAVENER

My wife, a pastry chef, tells me that when she bakes bread, she adds yeast as an ingredient – so that the bread will rise. In this way, yeast is a *leavener*.

She tells me that when she adds the yeast to the flour mixture, that the yeast begins to feed off the natural carbohydrates (sugars) in the flour. This produces carbon dioxide and alcohol. The carbon dioxide gives the rise – it forces the gluten structure (the flour mixture) to stretch and expand. The alcohol enhances the flavor.

Similarly, discipline is the great leavener of our lives. When added to our other natural attributes and our person ingredients, we stretch and expand.

Consider that every great accomplishment by our heroes depended on some human characteristic. Mother Theresa will forever be known for an overwhelming ability to love and care for others. Charles Lindberg will be known for his trans-Atlantic flight. Albert Einstein for the Theory of Relativity. Tiger Woods for his unrivaled talent as a golfer. Shakespeare.

These are all examples that we're familiar with. None of these individuals were known, per se, for their discipline.

They were known for other qualities or for their extraordinary accomplishments.

What allowed these people to expand on their natural talents and abilities to the point of becoming immortal examples of perfection in their chosen profession? What fueled the personal growth required to follow their dreams?

If we believed that these great people, including our personal heroes, were just *born* with the "natural" ability to succeed, we'd be missing 99% of what it took for him to do what he did.

Let's take Leonardo da Vinci as an example. I'm not saying that God had nothing to do with his creative talents. I'm not saying that he wasn't genetically wired for creativity, either. I'm not saying that the right side of his cerebral cortex wasn't more fully developed than yours or mine. But what I am saying that his talents would have been completely irrelevant if he had never painted, sculpted, or written anything.

If Mother Theresa had never journeyed to distant lands to serve the poor, she would not have exemplified her natural charity for the less fortunate.

If Abraham Lincoln had never run for office (over and over) his picture wouldn't be on the penny, the map of the U.S. might look a lot different today, and you would never had heard mention of the Gettysburg address.

1%, or maybe even less, of what these people did, had anything at all to do with natural talent. I think it would be dishonest to say that these people weren't born with some degree of intrinsic ability. But it would also be a lie to say that you were born *without* any natural abilities. Whether you *use* and *develop* your abilities is the *only* relevant question.

Let me repeat that, because it bears repeating:

Whether we discipline ourselves to use our talents should be the focus of our energy. Not whether we were born with more of a talent than someone else, or with the talents that we really wanted, or with any noticeable talents at all.

Let's talk about trading for a moment. It's simply not relevant to ask *whether* you have any natural forex tading abilities. I can help you develop the ability to trade.

But, hey, once you throw yourself from the cliff and start trading on a live forex account, hopefully you've made a jump (safely) to the other side – not to the bottom. Hopefully, the strategy you took all that time to develop is going to be worth something. That's what <u>this</u> book is about. I want to talk to you about how to jump safely to the other side, and to do it better than anyone else.

Discipline will expand on your trading abilities. It will stretch you.

Thomas Edison, who patented 1,093 inventions, said that "Genius is one percent inspiration and 99 percent perspiration." He failed thousands of times before succeeding at inventing the incandescent light bulb. Discipline drove him to succeed despite initial failures. His discipline – he often worked over 20 hours per day – stretched his natural abilities. I suppose there were many inventors as inspired or intelligent as Edison. History proves that few were as disciplined.

My first important job came during college when I interviewed to become a supervisor of Italian language instruction at my university. I needed the money. I had recently become engaged to be married, and I had no idea how I could go to school and support my family unless I received an increase in pay. When the supervisor's job opened, I knew I had to get it.

I already spoke Italian. I had been a good Italian instructor. But I didn't have the "natural" ability to supervise. I certainly didn't have the natural ability to interview for the supervisor's job. So what did I do? First I made a list of everything I needed to succeed in this interview. Here's the list I made:

Meet boss. Find out what he looks for. Practice what he looks for until it feels natural. Play the game to win.

For the week leading to the interview, I talked to every other language supervisor I could find. I talked to everyone. I talked to the individual whom I was meant to replace. Having gathered as much information as I could, I started practicing the interview. Every night, I would grab anyone I could find and I would practice the answers to my interview questions. Some of these people had no idea what I was saying in Italian. But I must have practiced at least 20 times before the day of the interview. By that time, I was ready. I took that list and I disciplined myself to check off every entry. One night, I practiced in front of the same (poor) person at least 15 times. As I completed these tasks, I realized that my natural abilities were stretched. My comfort zone was expanding: I realized that I *could* interview for this job. That I did have the abilities necessary.

I aced the interview.[3] I got the job and I earned enough money to help support my small family.

Now let's talk about trading.

Before I started trading on the foreign exchange, I was in a similar predicament: the company I had founded wasn't doing well. My job was becoming unbearable at the same time that the company was headed into its 400th crisis. I had to make a decision on where to focus my efforts – I couldn't run the company *and* do something else. But I needed income, and I needed it right then.

I knew that it I focused, if I disciplined myself, I would be successful. I knew that if I spread out my efforts, I would fail.

---

[3] At the time, I had always been very, very nervous during interviews. But I remember than when I interviewed for this job, I was smiling the entire time. I was happy to be there interviewing, because I had prepared. I'm smiling now as I remember it, because it was one of the only times in my life that I've interviewed for a job and not been sweaty-palms-nervous.

I dropped everything and learned everything I could about the foreign exchange. Imagine stepping off into the dark, into the unexplored regions of your life, without a net. Well, that's what I did. A lot of people I was close to thought I was crazy. I knew that if I didn't dedicate myself completely, I wouldn't succeed. More on this later. For now, I want you to know that the first step in discipline is the following:

A disciplined person knows he must be willing to dedicate himself 100% to the success of a chosen venture. No matter what it takes, he's willing to endure.

Think of a time when you succeeded. Think of a time when you were able to accomplish something difficult, or important. How did you feel back then? How did you prepare for, or make it through, that moment?

Then ask yourself: What are you working on right now? Are you on the hunt for a job? A promotion? A better relationship? Whatever it is, discipline can help you expand and stretch your natural abilities. Right now, write down everything you would need to be successful at this endeavor:

_____

_____

_____

_____

_____

_____

Discipline will help you get all those things done. You might have to get up early, stay up late, or move out of your comfort zone. But as you do those things, you will realize that your talents are expanded.

If you make that list, and you dedicate yourself to doing everything it takes to accomplish your goal, your natural abilities will be stretched. And you'll be ready for the challenge.

PART 3: DISCIPLINE IS A CHOICE

Often when I speak with people, they tell me, "Rob, I know I should be more disciplined. But just knowing it isn't enough. I'm just *not a* disciplined person." If you have ever felt this way, then this chapter is for you.

Discipline is a choice. There is no such thing as a person *born* disciplined. There are just people who choose to pursue a life of discipline and those who don't.

Daniel Goleman, in his ground-breaking book, Emotional Intelligence, which you should read, discusses the "Marshmallow Experiment." At an early age, a set of children were told to sit at a table in a room for an hour, and were given one marshmallow. They were told that if they did not eat the marshmallow during that one hour, they would be rewarded with an entire bag of marshmallows. If they ate the single marshmallow, they wouldn't receive any more.

It turns out that the children, who at an early age had the discipline to resist the marshmallow, were more successful later in life in terms of financial wealth, education, and satisfying relationships.

When I first read this book (during law school), I thought to myself, "Well, so much for me. I'm sure I'd eat the one marshmallow *now*, let alone when I was five years old." I'll agree that, for some of us, it's not the most encouraging story.

But my message to you is that you feel like you can't resist the marshmallows of life, then you're in good company. Help is on the way. Take heart from this simple truth:

It's never too late to learn discipline!

So, if you feel like saying, "I wasn't *born* with discipline," then I feel like saying: I wasn't either! We weren't born with the ability to eat without help. We didn't leave the hospital and go buy cigars for our dad's friends. We learned those things. Likewise, we can learn discipline. If you can read this book, you can learn discipline. In fact, the decision you made to read it in the first place is part of your decision to do anything it takes to become successful at disciplining yourself. The fact that you've made it this far in the book is another sign. Believe me, there are a lot of people out there who want to be successful but who aren't willing to do whatever it takes to get what they want.

So, to summarize, you'll find that all of us were born with the *potential* to discipline ourselves. I'll also remind you that I'm not asking you to have as much discipline as a Marine drill sergeant. I'm asking you to develop as much discipline as you are able. Your greatness is achieved by increasing your discipline, not by reaching Charles Atlas' level of discipline. This bears repeating:

It's perfectly fine to emulate another's discipline, or learn from it. But you are not in a race or competition to acquire more of it than anyone else. You are only in a race against yourself. If comparing yourself to other people motivates you, then by all means do it. But be warned that there will always be someone else who appears to have more discipline or less discipline than you. You will always be happier if you simply strive to improve yourself, measuring your progress against your own abilities.

When my aunt completed her 400-page dissertation, one week before defending it, she breathed a sigh of relief and shut off her computer. The next day, when she awoke, she walked to her computer and – tried to turn the computer back on so she could print the dissertation.

And the computer bombed.

She gasped. Was the entire dissertation lost? Would she have to start writing all over? First tears, then fear.

What would she do?

Right there, she determined that she would borrow a friend's computer and start writing immediately. She faced all of those sorrows, all of those people she had treated – she faced them all over again as she started to write.

She finished on time. But she could have easily made a different choice.

My wife and I tried to have children for 6 years. Finally, one January evening, when we were just a week away from being certified to adopt by the state of West Virginia, we discovered that our greatest dream came true: she was pregnant. Two months later, the ultrasound showed that he was a boy. A month later, we decided him to name him after my father and I. We bought a crib, a stroller, clothes.

Five months later, we raced to the hospital at 1am because I couldn't detect a heartbeat when I leaned my ear against her womb.

An hour later we started to lose hope.

An hour after that the doctor told us that there was no hope for our son.

And later that same morning, on September 23, 2003, my wife had to give birth – naturally – to our dead son. Could she have chosen to give up? Sure. Would anyone have criticized her? Absolutely not. Instead of taking on a defeated attitude, my wife bravely cried and pushed and cried and pushed. The doctor had told her that under the circumstances, her labor would last 12 to 18 hours.

It lasted 2.

It took discipline for my wife to simultaneously lose hope that her dreams would come true on that day, but still give birth. It took discipline for her to trust that another child would come and not become furious with me, or with God, or with the doctors. This doesn't mean that she wasn't heartbroken. What I'm saying is that she made a conscious choice to discipline herself under the most difficult of circumstances.

Choosing discipline isn't easy. But it's worth it.

PART 4: DISCIPLINE IS MORE PRECIOUS THAN GOLD

Discipline is a miracle more valuable than gold because it's what *gets* you the gold. We've all heard stories about the gold miner who was just a foot or an inch away from the vein of gold before he gave up.

One of my favorite quotes comes from Harriet Beecher Stowe, the author of *Uncle Tom's Cabin*. She said:

When you get into a tight place and everything goes against you, till it seems as though you could not hang on a minute longer, never give up then, for that is just the place and time that the tide will turn.

In the end, I'm only writing and distributing this book so that I can help you, in some small way, to achieve what you want to achieve. If you look back on your life to the most happy moments, and wish for that feeling again – but don't know quite how to get it – then read on. We're going to pick up the pace on the path to discipline right now.

PART 5: THE FOUR ENEMIES OF DISCIPLINE

I think I've started a work-out program at least every year for the past 10 years. Now, that's not so extraordinary, is it? For sure, you know someone who has done the same. Failure at implementing an exercise regimen is commonplace. But what makes my failure in this arena so infuriating is that 12 years ago, I implemented an exercise program and lived up to it for 2 years! Somewhere along the way, I lost my discipline. I stopped working out.

One of the greatest questions in my life has been to understand not only why I never finished a project, completed a goal in the first place, but how in the world I can screw something up that *I've already proven possible before.*

Have you ever discovered a great trading strategy, implemented it successfully, and then one day just blown the whole thing to pieces by violating the strategy? I've done that before.

The problem lies in the lack of Discipline. And the absence of Discipline is always the result of the *appearance* of one of these Four Enemies.

Enemy One: Fear. We fear the ability to achieve what we set out to do, so we never try in the first place (failure from the start) or we simply give up along the way (failure midstream). Much has been made of the theoretical "fear of success" vs. the "fear of failure," and frankly, I've experienced both kinds, plus some others for good measure. Understanding the different kinds of fear is an excellent way to identify which you struggle with the most.

Fear of Failur.. This is probably the most common. This is the reason that salespeople fail to make their cold calls, and it's why shy people end up really lonely. If you struggle with a fear of failure, you're in good company. Fear of failure also includes instances when we just stop trading because we're afraid we've lost so much of our account value that the only way to stop losing is to not trade at all.

Fear of Success. This sounds a bit silly at first, but many of us live with a fear of what will happen if we succeed. One of the saddest moments in my life was when I realized that a person I love dearly was so afraid of having to accept success that she decided to sabotage her own victories. People who fight this fear often are worried that if they are successful, the world will expect more of them than they are able to provide.

Fear of the Unknown. Most of us have felt this when we get lost while driving. Once in high school, I summoned the courage to beat back fear of failure: I asked a beautiful, smart girl on a date. She accepted. On the night of the date, I was so afraid of what to do on a date that I never even picked her up. When I saw her at school, I avoided her. I never spoke another word to her. Enough said about that experience.

When you're afraid of what you don't know, you're more inclined to *almost* implement a new trading strategy. For instance, you'll open a live account and then not quite follow through on everything you learned from the demo account experience. You're afraid of what will happen if you just let the strategy fly with real money. That's a good way to lose your live account.

There are many other examples of types of fears that we encounter. Succumbing to these fears gives one a sense of comfort. A salesperson, when he decides to not make a difficult cold call, feels more comfortable. Of course, he has succumbed to an enemy of discipline. In this way, each of us trades the chance for success each time we succumb to these fears.

Giving into these fears doesn't make you more comfortable in the long term, however. My first job after law school was my big introduction to the world of finance, as I worked as a headhunter for top-level financial professionals. I did very well at that job because every morning when I walked in the door to work, I picked up the phone immediately and started making as many cold calls as I could. Every evening I made a list of cold calls to make the next day. I was uncomfortable when I made the calls. I felt very comfortable, however, when I closed deals *because* I had been willing to make those calls. On the other hand, in 9 months of work I watched the four people that sat around me fail miserably – they didn't make as many calls, and they eventually felt far less comfortable.

Enemy 2: Distraction. Distraction is the experience of trading what you should be thinking about for what is more convenient or urgent. It's when you daydream when you ought to be driving (this is bad); it's *not* when you daydream while you're taking a Geometry test (this is completely natural *and* harmless).

Distraction is not bad all the time. I think allowing ourselves to become distracted on a regular basis has some merit; in fact, I find a lot of comfort in allowing myself to play a couple of rounds of a video game in the middle of the workday. Letting yourself go for a while can be healthy.

But it can also be destructive.

After the fifth grade – and the year that I had decided, once and for all (at age 10) that I was going to be a writer – I promptly forgot everything that I had decided. I entered the sixth grade, I started having to switch classes. I discovered that girls existed (although they did a fine job of ignoring my existence for the next, well, forever). Instead of writing, which I still loved, I let the talent slip. For at least two more years I didn't pick up a pen and paper.

I lost critical time when I did that. When I became distracted and allowed myself to pursue other activities, instead of just writing for a few minutes a day, I established a precedent. During that time, I did **think** of writing. But I started to become used to other things. Over time, those other things commanded my attention. Writing was all but forgotten.

Distraction is especially bad for you if you succumb to it immediately after making an important decision. Sadly, we're all quite good at this. There are so many shows, people, projects, and goals that are competing for our attention. We don't always succeed in keeping our eye on the ball.

I have trained hundreds of forex traders across the globe, and not a few of them have bragged to me about what kinds of things they can do while trading – they play with the kids, balance the checkbook, work at a day job, or some other activity. In every case I have advised the trader to stop trying to do two things at once. For a while, putting one foot in the world of trading and the other someplace else won't be a big deal. But when the stakes get higher, you need to be focused.

Because trading is Web-based, many traders succumb to online pornography while trading. This practice is not only repugnant, but it's destructive to your trading profits.

The exercises in this book will help you stay focused on what's important. And they won't interfere with your natural right to completely disregard responsibilities every once in a while.

Enemy 3: Delay. They say that necessity is the mother of invention – that when we're under pressure to produce, we become more innovative. I propose that procrastination is the mother of regression.

As I've toured the country and spoken to traders, I've been told that procrastination is just a *system* that works well for some people. I've been told that sometimes, you just can't think clearly about a project until the very last minute. I accept that as valid. It's happened to me many times. At the last minute I seem to have the mental resources to complete a project.

If that's a valid point, then why would delay be an enemy of discipline?

Procrastination, or delay, is the act of avoiding what you know you must do. It doesn't build character. It saps you of character. It might bring out a lot of creativity, but it robs you of precious time, and you subject yourself to unnecessary pressure.

I'll put it as simply as possible: when you procrastinate, you might find a huge resource of energy to complete a project – but you don't have any time to review what you've done. I think you and I are prone to do some of our best work under pressure. I also think that we're sometimes prone to do some of our *worst* work under pressure.

Now, if you're absolutely, positively, motivated to do your very best work at the last minute, then I suggest that you follow the advice of Jerry Hirschberg, the designer responsible for many of Nissan's most innovative vehicles. He says that if you're motivated and inspired by tight deadlines, then you should set preliminary deadlines. I think it's a fantastic exercise, and we'll talk more about it later.

This applies to trading, too. There is a pervasive belief amongst traders (both equity and forex traders) that time of day matters little when trading – that you can make profits any time of the day. So, for U.S.-based traders, they decide that they don't have to get up in the middle of the night to catch the European and Asian markets. Well, this is a form of procrastination: trading sleep for profits. If you want to be successful at trading on the foreign exchange, you have to be willing to consistently get up and get going at the same time every day.

Worse yet, many traders I meet with have lost substantial amounts of money by staying in a losing trade for too long – procrastinating the exit. This can drain your account faster than anything. It can tear you to pieces, too. If you have this problem, or the opposite (exiting too quickly), increased discipline will give you everything you need in order to make better, more profitable trading decisions.

Enemy 4: Despair. There simply doesn't exist a more pernicious enemy to discipline. We are all susceptible to some form of despair, and we've all battled it. Some of us have been more successful than others. But when it gets hold of us, it saps of us of our discipline faster than anything else. Here's a letter I received that makes the point better than I ever could:

I always dreaded coming home, but on the day that I received my 12th grade report card I was more fearful than ever. My dad expected the very best in me – this was the same man who resolved his problems with my mother by yelling, by breaking furniture, and by threatening to do things much worse.

I carried in my hand three Cs and two As. I knew that if I revealed the report card to my father, that anything was bound to happen. But I also knew that if I didn't show it to him, he was going to find out about it anyway.

I thought about running away from home that day.

Instead, I showed him the report card.

And he beat me. I let him hit me. He chased me down the steps of our house (no one else was home) and he told me that I was stupid. He said a lot of other things, but when he told me I was stupid, well, that hurt more than anything else. He chased me down the stairs and beat me with his boot.

I'll pause here and ask you: what would your reaction be?

When he was finished, he trailed off into the master bedroom and left me in the hall. He was still yelling at me from his room. I didn't know what to do. I didn't know if I should throw myself from my bedroom window, run to my friend's house, or call the police.

Instead of doing any of those things, I simply returned to my bedroom and studied. No one was going to call me stupid.

*I have since graduated from medical school. My dad remained violent. He eventually lost custody of my brothers and sisters. But I seriously look back on the day I brought that report card home, and I realize that **he's** the one that failed. It turns out I wasn't stupid.*

Our reactions to the bad things that happen to us are completely within our control. The things that happen to us – well, that's an entirely different story: sometimes we control our circumstances and sometimes, as in the letter above, we don't. Choosing to lose hope would have left the letter-writer with hardly the will to live. Now she's living a life of care – tending to the needs of the sick. We are all better off that she decided to reject the enemy of depression.

When you trade currency online for a living, you're going to get burned eventually. At times like that, it's easy to lose hope. When you lose hope, you lose everything. You've beaten yourself. The best solution to this is to get the help you need to improve your discipline and your trading abilities.

It's not enough to just have a positive attitude, and falsely believe that everything will turn out okay. You have to get up and do something.

The Smoking Monkey.

Ah, what a trade!

Chapter Seven

The 10 Rules of Trading

Rule #1: Never Lie to Anyone.

Never lie to yourself about anything. Or to anyone else, for that matter. When people tell me that they are honest with themselves but can't be completely honest with others (for whatever reason), I think they're just complicating the whole problem. There is no difference between lying to yourself and lying to someone else.

If you feel comfortable lying in general, that's going to catch up with you in the trading world. What happens when you lose a ton of money one day? Are you going to be tempted to hide that from others? From a loved one? If you can't face up to your greatest weaknesses in life, how are you going to face up to huge losses in trading? And if you don't face up to those losses, how are you ever going to improve?

Rule #2: Bank Your Gains.

Greed will kill you so fast in this business that you won't even know what hit you. Traders online or in print brag about how much they made on one trade. The ones who can make 100 pips on a trade are the ones who post their comments on discussion boards. Those are the visible guys, but you should know that those are the guys who play close to the edge. The harder you play, the harder you fall.

We hear a lot about the rule of expectation and building a system with a 1:1 or a 1:4 ration or whatever. This is all well and good, but all I want to know is whether you are willing to take profit off the table when you've got it. Why do we get upset when we take profit but the trade continues to make more money? You should never feel upset about that.

1 pip of profit is always better than any loss. Period. Never forget that.

And don't forget – until you get the money into your regular checking account (you know, the one you can pay bills out of), the profit is all on paper. Take your gains!

Rule #3: Take Your Time.

Never rush into a trade on emotion. Get up early enough – or stay in front of the charts long enough – to get a feel for the market (see #4 below) before you do anything.

What if you see the most stupendous trade ever, the most amazing opportunity you've ever seen in the whole history of the world? Well, unless you've been sitting in front of the charts for at least 15 minutes to 1 hour, then you should probably let it go.

Racing into a trade is usually the result of emotion taking over. You never want to trade based on emotion. Usually trades based on emotion lack the kind of analysis that goes into profitable trades.

Remember, that the market comes and goes. There is always another opportunity. You will get another chance. If you enter a trade and it's one that you entered based on emotion, then you should strongly consider backing out.

Backing out isn't failure. You don't want to hold on for a long time to a trade that you know was entered for stupid reasons. Exiting an emotional trade is a disciplined move.

And you know that every victory for discipline brings you closer to trading for a living.

Rule #4: Trust Your Feelings.

Ben Kenobi gave this advice to Luke Skywalker, and all Luke could say is "Well, I can't see with the blast shield down," or, in other words, "I can't read where the markets are going unless I see everything."

Well, you're never going to have all the information. You're always going to be missing some piece of information. You're never going to get to peek past the far right edge of the charts.

In other words, you're going to have to stay in touch with your feelings about the market. And you're going to have to act on them.

If you have been a diligent student of the markets, then you have nothing to worry about. Look at the charts. Check them in different time frames and using all the tools you've learned to use. Check with trusted analysts.

Then ask yourself, "How do I feel about the market today?" You'll be surprised at how right you can be if you just listen closely.

Rule #5: Successful Trading is Boring.

Learning to trade successfully requires a lot of time reading and in front of the computer. There will be days you don't trade at all, even though you spent four hours watching the charts.

While making money never gets boring, watching the charts is never much fun. Especially if you have to wait more than a few hours for a good trade.

Learn to pass the time by learning more and more about the charts you're looking at. Watch them in different time frames simultaneously. Test different tools and indicators that you have never used before. Go back in time and see how new strategies would work.

You can't necessarily make the time less boring, but you can certainly use that time to your advantage.

Rule #6: Exits are More Important than Entries.

If you keep modest goals and do your homework before you trade, then where you get in isn't the big deal.

Where you get *out*, not where you get *in,* determines your profit. That seems so easy to understand but many traders don't think about it.

Most traders are worried about how far the trade goes against them and start to feel quesy as soon as the trade turns unprofitable.

Great traders don't worry about that. They worry about whether the pair is reaching levels that bring out a stop loss. They also worry about whether they have taken all the profit out of a trade.

You should think more about where to get out rather than where to get in.

Rule #7: How Much You Risk Matters Most.

More than anything else, how much you risk determines how long you can stay in the game. If you've ever lost your entire account on one trade (or just a few trades), then you've risked too much. You can't risk so much that a small move against you takes you out of the market.

Many traders get involved in the forex market because they want to make a lot of money quickly. This requires you to either start with a lot of money or risk a lot on each trade.

You should never risk more than 10% on each trade, and you should never use that much equity unless you feel very, very confident about your abilities. The name of the game is survival. You will survive longer if you can whether the big swings in the market.

Rule #8: Keep a Journal.

You should keep a trade journal and it should record, for every trade:

1. Currency pair.
2. Long or short.
3. Entry price.
4. Stop order.
5. Limit order.
6. Why you entered the trade.
7. Exit price.
8. Pips gained.

This information will help you build a history of good trades. You'll make better trades if you have to keep track of them. You'll have to convince yourself on paper of every move you make. Don't worry about whether this will slow you down – you can always fill in parts of the journal after each trade.

Rule #9: Get a Coach.

I've said this a zillion times before. But it's so important to get a coach. You should report to this coach on a regular basis about your progress. You should show your coach your trading journal and be totally honest about your mistakes.

Your coach doesn't have to be knowledgeable about trading currency, but it will help. Most importantly, this person will help you:

1. Stay committed to a system.
2. Recognize your mistakes.
3. Plan for correcting mistakes.
4. Stay humble even when you are successful.
5. Stay grounded when you lose money.

Rule #10: Never Overtrade.

It's too easy to make a few good trades and then start entering tons more. It's also real easy to churn, to get out of trades too early, then back out of those trades and into more and more …

This cycle can only hurt you, and it's symptomatic of traders who are not satisfied with consistent profits built up over time.

When you are a successful trader, you will occasionally feel the urge to bet the house, or trade a whole bunch, because you're absolutely sure that you know where the market is going. These are the days that you should enter a regular order just like you always do, and then watch the trade turn profitable, and then get out. Just handle it like any other day.

If you start to overtrade, then talk to your coach. Get yourself back in line!

Chapter Eight

Oh, crap!
I just lost my entire account!

So, you lost some money trading currency. That's what the forex is all about, right? Money. Somebody wins and somebody loses. I lost 90% of my first account in 72 hours. Whooohoo! That was a rush. Did wonders for my self-esteem.

The real question to ask yourself after you lose money is: *what am I going to do about this?* And that's exactly what I am going to talk with you about right now.

Most people, when they lose some money, feel the temptation to do one of three things:

1. Panic
2. Give up
3. Get revenge

Most traders have been taught that "panic" and "trading" are not two words that go together very well. And it's obvious that if you give up, you should not even be reading this book right now. You should go get a book about selling your stuff on eBay, to try to at least get back some of those losses.

But revenge? What about revenge?

I am here to tell you that it's perfectly ok to want to get revenge. And I am going to show you how to impose a savage beating on the currency market, to take back what was rightfully yours (until you made the lame mistake of not having a stop loss).

Why You Lost Money #1:
You risked too much on one or more trades.

You probably started trading currency for the same reason I did: to make money. While that's a worthy goal, and one that you're likely to reach, it's just not wise to try and make a year's worth of profits in one trade.

Most of us, at one time or another, have risked 50% or more of our account on one or more trades. Most of us try that on our demo accounts, and then we start to feel invincible (look! See what I can do! I can double my money in just a week!). Of course, this led you to try something similar in your live account. That was a bad idea (but you already know that now).

Solution: Never risk more than 1% of your account on a single trade. Preferably less. Yes, you read that correctly. When you are just learning how to do this, you want to risk very little on each trade. The time will come for you to risk a greater percentage on each trade. That time is not now.

This is a money-management solution. If you don't put a lot of money on the roulette table, you can have a lot of your money taken *off* the roulette table. I guess that's a bad analogy, however. You should never play roulette, anyway. It's a game meant to always take away from you, no matter how good you think you are.

Why You Lost Money #2:
You set a lame stop loss, or none at all.

Setting a stop loss is like zipping up your pants in the morning. It's not required, but you can feel really embarrassed, really quickly, if you don't do it. To tell you the truth, you could conceivably set a stop loss 100 pips wide just to get 10 pips. If you are not risking more than 1% of your account on the trade, it doesn't much matter. I have done this before. I don't do it any longer, because that is a dumb risk:reward ratio. The point here is that you *must* set some type of stop loss so that if the market really gets wild, that you don't get crushed.

Why You Lost Money #3:
You traded on emotion, not reality.

You and I sometimes get a good string of trades put together, and then we start walking around like we're the Warren Buffet of forex (we're not). A good thing to remember at a time like that is this: *you are not the Warren Buffet of trading – and the longer you keep up that attitude, you're more likely to end up looking like the ENRON of forex.* Bring yourself back down to earth before every trade. Make sure you take your time before every trade. Make sure that if you're making what you believe to be a "sure bet," then you better not risk more than 1% of your capital and set appropriate stop loss orders. Especially at the beginning of your trading career. You can start to risk more when you learn more. When you have a track record.

Why You Lost Money #4:
You just started trading with real money.

Your first trades with real money are the most amazing opportunities to lose money. You and I both did it – one week after I opened my first live account, I lost 90% of my account. I felt like crawling under a rock. Or smashing my head with one. It's like magic: open a live account, lose money.

Realize that no matter how good you were on a demo account, you're going to trade on emotion as soon as you open a live account. Mostly, you're going to feel afraid to follow the same hair-brained strategy that you used when you were on the demo account. Here are five ideas that will help you avoid this:

1. Open your next live account with $2,000 or less. Trade for less than $1 per pip.
2. If you built a strategy / system while on a demo account, use it! It worked then, right?
3. If you didn't build a system already, use that new small account to build one.
4. Don't be afraid of losing money. Be afraid of making stupid trades.
5. NEVER, EVER, EVER, EVER trade when you're emotional. Email me if this is a problem for you and I can suggest some things that helped me: rob@robbooker.com.

Why You Lost Money #5:
Something weird happened.

Well, it's true: sometimes the market does things that it's not supposed to do. Take Japanese intervention in the Yen – it's not supposed to happen in a perfect world, but it does, and it can really throw off your perfect short trade. Or your forex dealer, like Refco, declares bankruptcy. These are the unpreventables, as I call them, and they don't happen as often as we suspect. When you get burned by a totally unpredictable movement in the market, just sit back, relax, and ask yourself: did you only risk a small amount of your capital? Did you have a stop loss? If you had a stop loss and you only risked a small portion of your account, you will be just fine.

Why It's Going to Be OK #1:

You're going to learn why you lost money. If you lost more than 10% of your account on one trade, then you did something wrong. You goofed. It's okay, just don't do it again. Take a day off from trading. Step back.

Write down why you entered the trade.
Write down why you exited the trade.
Write down what you should have done differently.

NOT studying your worst moments is like smashing your thumb with a finger, and then smashing it again. And again. I have worked with traders who have been making the same mistakes for more than a year – have blown more than one account – and then when they spend a week studying the reasons for their trades, they become profitable traders.

YOU HAVE TO STUDY YOUR BAD TRADES. YOU HAVE TO LEARN FROM THEM.
IF YOU DO, YOU WILL START MAKING MONEY.

Why It's Going to Be OK #2:
Why did you enter the trade?
Did you enter the trade on a spur of the moment, emotional feeling? Write everything down. If you feel like you did everything right, that you entered the trade for all the right reasons, then maybe you didn't stay in the trade long enough. If you have NO IDEA what happened, maybe you should write me – or someone who has been trading longer than you have. Ask them to look at the charts. Ask them what you could have done differently.

You should get in the habit of keeping a trade journal. The journal should include the following information:

Time of entry and type of trade (Buy, Sell, Pair, Lot size). Stop loss and limit orders.

Why you entered the trade. For example: "5 EMA crossed below the 30."

Time and price of exit, and any gain/loss.

Why It's Going to Be OK #3:
Why did you exit the trade?

Many traders who give a reason for a trade entry don't give a reason for the exit. The best reason to exit the trade is that it's profitable and you want the money in your account. The worst reason to exit a trade is because it's going against you and you don't know what else to do.

You have to have a plan for the trades that go against you! Before you start trading as a career, or with any substantial money, you should make a plan for what you're going to do if a trade goes south. Some questions you need to answer:

How far am I willing for this trade to go against me? Sometimes traders set a stop loss that's too wide or not wide enough, and then they disregard it anyway.

What are the criteria for realizing that the trade was not a good idea? Here, it's not enough to say, "I'm losing money." I mean, if you enter trades on an oscillator or indicator, do you exit based on those tools as well? What signals are given for a trade exit?

And last of all, you want to ask yourself: *under what circumstances will you raise or lower your stop loss and your limit orders?* The answer here should be that you will never adjust your stop unless you have put it so far away that you are risking more than a small fraction of your account.

Why It's Going to Be OK #4:
What would you do differently next time?

I once got a bad haircut: at the end, nearly all of my hair was gone. I vowed to never let that happen again. Talk about (with a friend who trades) or write down what you would have done differently. Would you have avoided entering the trade altogether? Would you have waited longer – for example, if the position eventually turned profitable, you have learned that sometimes the only thing separating you from profits is time. Would you have double-checked the indicators? Would you have looked closer at candlestick patterns? Asked an expert?

Once you decide what you would have done differently, then find someone who can help you keep your goal to act differently next time. Find a fellow trader who will double-check your trades. Set goals and get someone to help you keep them. Trading requires discipline and you can increase your discipline by working together with someone.

Why It's Going to Be OK #5:
Get revenge.

Now create a list of goals for your forex trading – make the list as short as possible, but you should probably include as one of your goals "Never make the same mistake I just made ever again." Once you've written your goals, you should also consider making a complete trading plan. That plan would include rules that you follow on getting in and out of trades, indicators that you watch, and maximum losses that you are willing to withstand before exiting a trade. It would also include a method for follow up (including your trading journal).

Now, take those goals. And implement them. Get mad about your loss. I *hate* losing money. Hate it as much as anything else. Do you? If so, channel that anger and become more disciplined. Channel it and develop new goals. Channel it and commit to change your trading habits so that you can make money. Don't be afraid to get revenge. But, as a good leader in battle, plan for it. Study it out. *And then attack.*

Unhelpful things to say to your spouse after a 300 pip loss, described by actual Anne Murray song titles.

"Sweet Little Jesus Boy"
"Lord I Hope This Day is Good"
"Hold Me Tight"
"Nobody Loves Me Like You Do"
"Could I Have this Dance"
"Broken Hearted Me"
"We Don't Make Love Anymore"

Chapter Nine

5/13/62

She was the first girl I thought I liked, or loved, or whatever. She sat next to me in a 7th grade class. I don't remember much about the class, mostly because I was spending so much time concentrating on Carrie. Most of the time, she was my friend. Except when we were outside of class.

Outside of class, she paid no attention to me. She ignored me. If she ever talked to me, she made fun of me, refused to spend time with me (or even admit I existed). Of course this only made matters worse. All of this only made me want her more. Carrie moved away after the 7th grade.

5 years later I found myself standing behind her at the market.
Every feeling I'd ever had for her returned instantly.

I was so entranced that I watched her as she left the drugstore, got into her car, and pulled out of the parking lot. Just when I thought that she neither remembered me, or even noticed me, she turned around, rolled down her window, and blew me a kiss. My heart jumped into my throat and I felt weak.

I never saw Carrie again.

You know what a pip is already. Do you know that most forex traders spend their careers chasing after pips in the same way I chased after Carrie's attention? She never gave it to me, unless (at the end) it was to blow me a teasing goodbye kiss. She had received all the benefit from my attention and never gave anything back except a blow to my selfesteem. Gosh, that sounds a lot like when I first traded currency – and the pips teased me until they simply moved away in the end, with a good-bye kiss.

Have you ever watched the market and wondered why the harder you tried, the more quickly the pips distanced themselves from you? I remember when I first started trading that the market would move away from me and I would begin to think: it's moving. Why is it moving away from me? Couldn't it just as easily move in my direction?

For a while, I made money on gut decisions. I'd make some progress, a few pips or more a day, but never really understand the signals. For instance, I'd make a profit just barely, and watch in horror / relief as the market swung the opposite way right after I exited the trade.

Or I'd enter a trade, lose a bunch of pips, and then exit the position at a loss – only to watch the market swing back in my favor. Only, of course, the position was closed and all I could do was sit there and watch, just like I had stood in the parking lot of the drugstore, watching Carrie blow that goodbye kiss.

WHAT I LEARNED

Until you're no longer impressed with pips – no longer frightened by them, nor infatuated by them, not in love with them, no longer simply hating them – they won't give you the time of day. The acquisition of pips is your only goal in the currency market. But pips are fickle and if you pursue them full of emotion, you're going to get
burned.

I learned in the drugstore that day 20 years ago that Carrie would have paid attention to me if I had simply ignored her every once in a while. If I had been able to get my feelings under control. If I'd been able to act cool instead of like a freak. If I'd been able to calmly make a plan, stick to it. But I could do none of those things. My emotions took hold of me and turned me into an idiot.

It's the same for pips. We all want them. We all want as many of them as we can get. But some of us are willing to risk everything for just a few of them. We'll chase after them like a 12-year old boy. And you know what? They don't give a damn about you and me.

This chapter will present a plan for learning about pips, where they're going, what they're about to do, and then arm you with a strategy that once implemented, can take a lot of the emotion out of trading.

Your goal will be to:

1. Enter positions as soon as a particular signal is given.
2. Exit the position as soon as a particular signal is given.

The payoff will be:

1.   The emotion should be gone from the trading.
2.   You will enter and exit trades with discipline and focus.
3.   You will get about 25 pips on the good trades. Maybe 30 and maybe even 50. There will be more winning trades than losing trades. The average loss will be about 25 pips.

ATTITUDE IS 99% OF SUCCESSFUL TRADING

Developing the right attitude about your trading is most of the work. Once you get your attitude (your discipline) under control, you're going to have more pips than you know what to do with. So much has been written about this that you'd think that you've already heard enough about it. I've written about it elsewhere, too1, but I've got to stress that no technique or strategy is worth more than the discipline you have to implement it.

The 5/13/62 strategy requires discipline. This is the most powerful personal characteristic you can acquire. Period. It will earn you more money and success than any other attitude or personality trait. If you're low on discipline, please take the time to consider what I'm saying:

In trading, discipline simply means two things:

1. Enter a position as soon as your system triggers an entry signal.
2. Exit the position when your system triggeres an exit.

If you do not acquire discipline, this system will not work for you.

No trading system will work for you. But this isn't a book about discipline. In fact, this book assumes that you have discipline, or you're willing to acquire in order to implement a profitable trading system.

So, for the purpose of this discussion, and for the testing of this strategy, please be disciplined – even as you practice.

EXPONENTIAL MOVING AVERAGES ARE THE KEY

They are the core element of this strategy. From the beginning you should understand that I didn't invent the 5/13/62 strategy. At least I don't think I did. There are some extras that I add in, but essentially, all of this information is available elsewhere. That said, I believe that most of the people that write about forex have a way of putting you and I to sleep.

So maybe this is the first time you've heard about it, but in any event, I'll try to keep it interesting.

Here's where we start. With a chart:

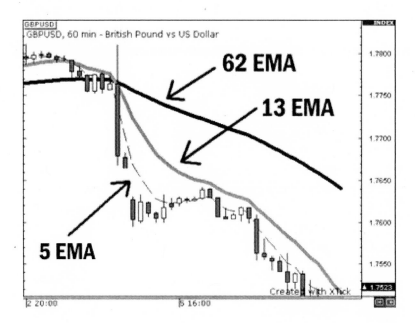

On the chart above, there are three moving averages that I identify with snazzy arrows. If you are having problems sorting out which moving average is which, I advise you to poke your eyeballs out with a pen.

If you have not poked out your eyeballs, you can easily see that when the 13 crosses below the 62, it seems like we are in a downward trending situation.

The inverse is also true (although we cannot see it in the chart above): if the 13 crosses above the 62, it seems like we are in an upward moving trend.

That's not quite everything, so we need to move on and do some more investigation.

CAN WE JUST TRADE CROSSOVERS?

The question arises: if those statements about upward and downward trends are true, then why not just sell a currency pair every time that the 13 crosses below the 62?

The answer is a that I have backtested (mechanically, by programming trading software) the system of simply buying when the signals cross above and selling when the signals cross below. There are even companies that build trading robots that will automatically buy and sell when these signals are given. But, as much as I'd like to say differently, it's not that easy.

There are all types of false signals (crosses that happen but that don't turn profitable). Here   are   some   other principles of this strategy, divided in three sections: entering the trade, staying in the trade, exiting the trade. The principles of each section will help you maximize your gains and minimize your losses.

But first, a quick look at the tools you'll need.

Charting Software.   You are going to need to be able to view candlestick charts, as well as moving averages. Charting programs are plentiful and free these days, so this is not a problem. Here are some charting programs I have used in the past. Some are free and others are not:

> Metatrader
> Xtick (what I use now)
> eSignal
> Oanda

The 30 Minute or 60 Minute Chart. I have used the 15 min, the 2 Hour, the 4 Hour, and even the daily charts with this system. I recommend that you study this system with the shorter time frame charts, like the 15 or 30 or 60 minute, so that you can see lots of examples of this system in action. This means that you will be able to practice much more frequently (because 15 minute candles form more frequently than 1hr/4hr/daily candles).

Moving Averages. Your charting software will automatically calculate the moving averages for you. But to get set up, you need to plot (as I did above) the 5, 13, and 62 EMAs on your 30 minute chart. If you do not know how to plot moving averages on your charts, then it would be a good idea to back up a bit, and spend a day or so learning how to use your charts.

PART 1: MAKING THE TRADE

Below you'll find the principles behind making good trades. And avoiding the bad ones. These are guidelines. Good trades based on these guidelines are the result of applying them enough times that you begin to get a feel for the market. I want to emphasize that you can change these rules. You can manipulate them. You will be most successful when you make this "your own," by adjusting so that you feel most comfortable.

Holidays and other bad days. Try not to trade on holidays, especially U.S. holidays. It's best to stay out of the market on those days and catch up on time with your family, see a movie, adjust the metal rod that was placed in your back, insert a metal rod in your back, or fire up the barbie-q and roast some weenies. Or you can back test your strategies. It's also best to never, ever, ever, enter a trade past 14:00 GMT on a Friday.

On holidays and late on Fridays, the market is unpredictable and might not move enough to give you any profit. Or it might move 50 points in one direction just for the heck of it, and then move back. Of course it might move a zillion pips, but that's the exception rather than the rule. Then you're stuck in what might become a losing position, but meanwhile, you're losing money to premiums/interest paid to your broker. This is a good time to shove a metal rod into your spine.

After 13:00 Eastern US Time. This is when the market slows down, and there can be a lot of false breakouts. Avoid trading during these times, especially on the shorter time frame charts.

Please take my advice and just stay out of the market, with this system, at these times. You may lose some opportunities, but you will lose (also) the chance of getting trapped in a motionless or unpredictable market.

Other systems, long term systems in particular, can work okay late on Fridays and on holidays. Those are systems that I teach in the live seminars and in the web-based training.

DNA Spirals. Often, a currency pair will find itself in a dorfwad, go-nowhere pattern that I call the "DNA Spiral." This is an apt name for the pair because the candles can spin back and forth around the EMAs, seemingly tangling them up into a twisting pattern. These are times that you do not want to trade. Here is an example below.

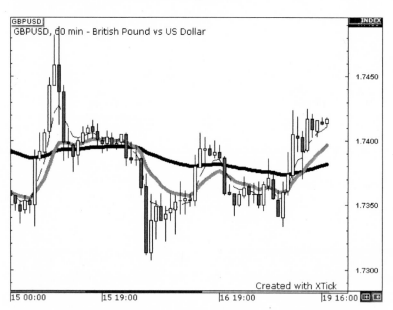

If I just told you when NOT to trade, we would only have a lame chapter, fit for burning or toilet paper. But now I am going to share with you when you need to become really excited about taking the trade.

When the 5 crosses the 13, and the 13 crosses the 62, and the 13 is at least 30-40 pips away from the 62, we are ready to trade. When this happens, we know that there is a higher probability that a trend has developed and we will have a chance to get in on the trend. Let's spend a moment and talk about this.

There is no reason why you can't just take every single crossover as soon as it happens. Meaning, you can avoid the bad hours and just wait, during the active market hours of 02:00 am – 11:00 am Eastern US, for the 5 to cross the 13 and the 13 to cross the 62. This actually does work. It can be a profitable trading system. But what I am asking you to do here is to actually consider waiting until a trend has shown itself – and then we will jump on the trend and take a trade.

Once we see the trend, we are ready to start thinking about a trade. And here is what we wait for: *We wait for the candles to fall back down and touch the 62 EMA. Then we buy.*

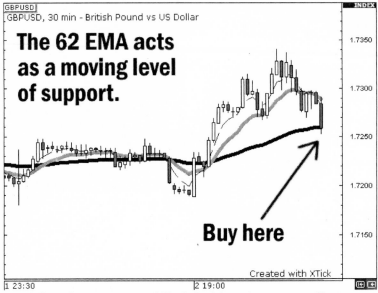

What about stops and limits? It's quite easy, really.

To contain our risk, we place a stop loss 25 pips below our entry price. The maximum stop I am willing to accept on a trade like this, on the 30 or 60 minute charts, is 40 pips. I won't show where we place the stop because I

We have more options on our profit target.

Set a profit target at the previous high that the pair made, before the candles fell back down to touch the 62 EMA. This will usually give us a profit target of at least 30 pips. On the example in the chart above, we have a profit target of approximately 80 pips. That's a very reasonable risk-to-reward setup.

Set a trailing stop of 20 pips and just let the trade run. This allows for the greatest amount of profit in fast moves in your favor.

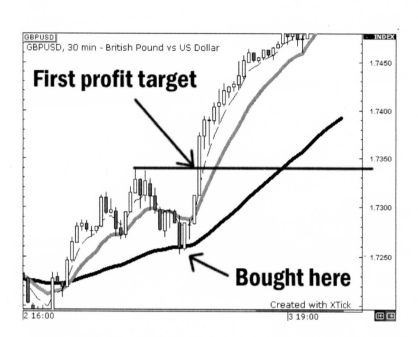

PART 2: DURING THE TRADE

So now what? You have a great trade going. Do you set it and forget it?

I believe that anyone who tells you to "set it and forget it" is appealing to your greedy desire for quick, easy profits without any work.

And right now, I would like to spend a few moments appealing to your desire for quick, easy profits without doing any work.

After the trade is open, and you have your stop loss and profit target set, it is a perfect time to go do something else. Have you ever noticed that if you stare at the charts, the candles never move? But if you go walk the dog, eat breakfast, start a rock band. I could play drums and this guy with really long hair at lead vocals, who smokes so his voice can be really raspy, but has family and drug problems and sometimes has to spend the night in jail, which eventually breaks up the band and leaves us 10 years later on VH1's "Where are They Now?"

If this disappoints you, or if you don't know whether a rock band is right for you, then feel free to watch the trade while it is open. That's perfectly ok, but just remember that many traders have experienced problems with peeing in their pants while their short term trades are open.

PART 3: WHAT NEXT?

I have worked with hundreds of traders, all over the world, and many of them have altered the 5/13/62 system to work for them. They get in earlier, or later, with different stops and limits. Or they trade on special days.

The point is that you can adjust and test this system to make it your own. And when you make it your own, that is when you start making some serious pips.

The Alpaca Chart Pattern.

Data

When trading redline breaks, you want to have enough space between the candles and the redline to fit at least one alpaca. You may be wondering, "WTF is an alpaca?" An alpaca is essential to fit between the candles, so that you can shave off the candle wicks, and the alpaca fiber and make some sweet sweaters. You also want to make sure there is enough volume to give you a good amount of profit on the redline break. Here you see that Ambush is able to cawl in the empty space between the candles and redline for some nice hanging out with pips time. This offers a prime situation for fiber and pip gathering. Alpacas are very pip friendly. Hmmmmmm.

Buy Time

| 7 19:00 | 9 19:00 | 11 19:00 | 15 19:00 | 17 19:00 | 21 23:00 | 23 19:00 | 25 19:00 | 29 19:00 |

©2006 Maxwell Fox and Rob Booker.

Chapter Ten

Why I Teach

People ask me all the time: if I am such a hot shot trader, why in the world am I spending time teaching other people? Would I not just spend all of my time trading?

I ask myself the same thing all the time, and I come back to the following answers.

First, I have more fun at teaching currency trading than anyone else. I might not be the best teacher, even. But I enjoy teaching this more than anything else. If you told me that I had to choose between managing money and education, I wuld choose education. I would simply trade my own account and teach.

Second, I don't have to give up trading when I teach. When I do a live seminar, I trade live in front of everyone. So I still get to take my trades.

Third, I get better ideas by teaching. When I collaborate with others in the web-based or live training that I do, I end up exchanging charts back and forth with other traders who follow the same systems that I do. This vastly improves my own ability to take the very best trades.

Fourth, I hire the best traders to work with me. I look for the very best traders, and I hire them to help me to manage money (either my own money or other people's money). By teaching other traders, I meet some of the very best currency traders. I get to see their performance close up.

Fifth, I may stop teaching. Despite all of the above, the basic concept is true: why am I still traveling and answering emails? The fact of the matter is that I won't be teaching forever. Maybe another year. Maybe 5 more. But I won't want to do it forever.

While I am still teaching, I hope that I get the chance to meet you, either by email or in person. It may take me a week or more, but I will answer your email. Keep in touch and let me know how you're doing. And don't forget to stop by and read my blog at:

http://www.piptopia.com